THE GUINNESS
CRICKET
QUIZ BOOK

Philip Bird

THE GUINNESS
CRICKET
QUIZ BOOK

Philip Bird

GUINNESS PUBLISHING

Published in Great Britain by Guinness Publishing Ltd, 33 London Road,
Enfield, Middlesex

All illustrations courtesy of Allsport UK Ltd

Designed by Stonecastle Graphics Ltd, Marden, Kent

Typeset in Rockwell by Ace Filmsetting Ltd, Frome, Somerset

Printed and bound in Great Britain by The Bath Press, Bath

'Guinness' is a registered trademark of Guinness Publishing Ltd

A catalogue record for this book is available from the British Library

ISBN 0–85112–598–0

CONTENTS

INTRODUCTION

The Guinness Cricket Quiz Book is a collection of cricketing quizzes set to test the knowledge of all fans of this great summer game.

Each quiz represents a different innings of 25 questions, each with a specific run value. At the end of every innings there is a multi-answer teaser, a chance to accumulate a number of singles to boost your score. Keep a note of all the innings scores on the page provided at the back of the book, and see how you fared overall.

Cricket has a habit of producing the unexpected – seemingly unbeatable records can be broken at any time. Indeed, this paradox is a quiz compiler's nightmare! All the 1600-plus questions here have been checked thoroughly, but I am sure all readers will forgive the odd fact that may have become outdated.

Philip E Bird

1

1 **SIX** Which country did England bowl out for just 45 at Old Trafford in June 1979?

2 **THREE** Which batsman scored 175 not out against Zimbabwe at Tunbridge Wells in the 1983 World Cup?

3 **SIX** Which ICC member country scored 455–9 off 60 overs versus Gibraltar at Rugeley in the 1986 ICC Trophy?

4 **FOUR** Which England batsman scored a fifty off just 34 balls in the match against Pakistan at Trent Bridge in August 1992?

5 **SIX** Which substitute wicket-keeper made four dismissals for New Zealand against Australia at Adelaide in November 1980?

6 **TWO** Who, at Old Trafford in May 1984, scored 189 not out for the West Indies in a Texaco Trophy game?

7 **SIX** Roy Fredericks was the first man to be dismissed in a World Cup final, but how was he out?

8 **FOUR** In the first World Cup competition, the West Indies beat Pakistan by one wicket with just two balls left. Who put on 64 with Deryck Murray for the last wicket?

9 **FOUR** Which left-arm swing bowler took 6–14 for Australia in the 1975 semi-final against England at Headingley?

10 **FOUR** Who scored 86 off only 55 balls in the 1979 World Cup final?

11 **SIX** Which New Zealander, playing against England in 1983, became the first bowler to concede 100 runs in a World Cup game?

12 **FOUR** Which bowler took 5–4 in 11 balls in the 1979 World Cup final?

13 **TWO** Which non-Test playing nation beat Australia by 13 runs at Trent Bridge in the 1983 World Cup?

14 **FOUR** Which Englishman scored the first century in a one-day international?

15   **SIX**   When England played Australia in the first one-day international at Melbourne in 1971, who was elected Man of the Match?

16   **FOUR**   Who, at Sydney in January 1987, scored 18 off the last over to steer England to a three-wicket win against Australia in a World Series game?

17   **FOUR**   Who caught and bowled Ian Botham in a World Series game in January 1987, but had to be carried off, helped by Botham, after tearing a hamstring?

18   **FOUR**   Who was named Man of the Match in the 1987 World Cup final?

19   **FOUR**   Which Englishman scored the most runs in the 1987 World Cup competition?

20   **SIX**   Who broke the record for the fastest fifty in one-day internationals, taking just 18 balls to reach the milestone for Australia versus Pakistan in 1990?

21   **SIX**   Which umpire stood in the first three World Cup finals?

22   **SIX**   Who was the first bowler to take a hat-trick in the World Cup?

23   **SIX**   Which Essex bowler coached Zimbabwe in the 1992 World Cup?

24   **THREE**   Which left-hander scored 113, the first one-day hundred for England against the West Indies in England, in the 3rd one-day international of 1991?

25   **FOUR**   Which Australian took the most wickets in the 1987 World Cup competition?

SINGLES (11) Name the England side that lost the 1987 World Cup final to Australia in Calcutta by 7 runs.

INNINGS SCORE:

BATTING I

1 **SIX** Who was the first batsman to score 5000 Test runs?

2 **FOUR** Who was the first batsman to play over 100 consecutive Test innings without scoring a duck?

3 **FOUR** Which current member of the Essex coaching staff was the first Englishman to score 1000 first-class runs in both 1989 and 1990?

4 **FOUR** Which Gloucestershire and Pakistan batsman was the first to score 1000 first-class runs in the 1981 season?

5 **SIX** Which Northamptonshire cricketer went 12 successive first-class innings in 1990 without scoring?

6 **FOUR** Which is the only side to score over 1000 runs in an innings *twice*?

7 **SIX** Who in 1967 became the first English Test player to score a century at each of the six main home Test grounds, when he hit 142 against Pakistan at the Oval?

8 **FOUR** Who scored 3429 runs in the 1949 season?

9 **THREE** Who opened the batting with Graham Gooch in the 1992 World Cup final?

10 **SIX** Who in 1990 became the first batsman since Alvin Kallicharran in 1984 to score a double century and a century in the same Championship match?

11 **FOUR** Who in 1990 became the tenth Australian to score two centuries in a Test, when he achieved the feat against Pakistan at Melbourne?

12 **SIX** Which Englishman was the first batsman to be not out in 50 Test innings?

13 **FOUR** Which England batsman came to the non-striker's end with his arm in plaster to steer England to a draw in the 2nd Test against the West Indies in 1963?

14 **THREE** Which England opener refused to walk when given out caught behind at Lahore in 1987?

15 **FOUR** Which overseas batsman scored hundreds and carried his bat in both innings versus Nottinghamshire in July 1989?

16 **SIX** Which Sri Lankan batsman scored a double century on his Test debut in 1987, only the third player to do so?

17 **FOUR** Which batsman hit 30 off a Kevin Sharp over in the Glamorgan versus Yorkshire Championship game in May 1987?

18 **FOUR** Who in 1990 became the first batsman to score four Test centuries at Lord's?

19 **THREE** Where did Tom Moody score the fastest ever hundred, in 1991?

20 **SIX** Which batsman has scored two separate hundreds in a match on the most occasions?

21 **FOUR** Which West Indian batsman scored five consecutive Test centuries in 1947–48 and 1948–49?

22 **TWO** Who was out playing the reverse sweep to Allan Border's first delivery of the 1987 World Cup final?

23 **FOUR** Which famous opening batsman scored 13 centuries in the 1971 season?

24 **SIX** Which future England captain scored 312 not out for the MCC under-25 side against North Zone at Peshawar in 1966–67?

25 **SIX** Which Australian opening batsman hit 32 off a Rosendorff over against Orange Free State on the Australians' 1969–70 tour of South Africa?

SINGLES (10) Give the ten different ways a batsman may be given out in first-class cricket.

INNINGS SCORE:

DERBYSHIRE

1 **THREE** Which current Derbyshire batsman holds the record for the most first-class centuries scored for the county?

2 **TWO** Which famous cricketer was specially registered by Derbyshire to play in John Player League games in 1972?

3 **FOUR** Which county beat Derbyshire to win the 1969 Gillette Cup final?

4 **FOUR** Which overseas bowler took 8–21 in a Nat West Trophy game for Derbyshire against Sussex in 1988?

5 **THREE** Which Test match captain replaced Ian Bishop as Derbyshire's overseas player for the 1991 season?

6 **FOUR** Who hit 241 not out, the third highest ever score for Derbyshire in Championship cricket, against Hampshire at Portsmouth in 1992?

7 **SIX** During the 1972 season only one Derbyshire player scored a first-class century. Who?

8 **FOUR** Which Derbyshire pace bowler was voted Young Cricketer of the Year in 1973?

9 **SIX** Which wicket-keeper made his Derbyshire debut in 1985 but can be seen playing football each winter, most recently keeping goal for York City and Scunthorpe United?

10 **THREE** Which former England all-rounder left the county for the second time at the end of the 1990 season?

11 **SIX** The Derbyshire captain from 1970–72 had the same name as one of their venues. Name him.

12 **TWO** Name the Derbyshire pace bowler who took 8–53 on his 20th birthday against Essex at Derby in August 1991, and was elected Young Player of the Year later that season.

13 **FOUR** Which England fast bowler was sent off the field for refusing to bowl against Yorkshire at Chesterfield in June 1973?

14 **FOUR** Which Derbyshire bowler was 12th man for the last two Tests against the West Indies in 1973?

15   **SIX**   Which pace bowler took four wickets in four balls in a John Player League game against Sussex at Derby in 1970?

16   **THREE**   Fast bowler Ole Mortensen has played international cricket for which country?

17   **FOUR**   Which former England opener captained Derbyshire to their 1981 Nat West Trophy win?

18   **SIX**   Which Scottish international was awarded his county cap in 1985?

19   **FOUR**   Which former England player left Yorkshire at the end of the 1981 season to join Derbyshire?

20   **TWO**   Which wicket-keeper scored his maiden first-class hundred for the county in 1981–20 years after his debut?

21   **FOUR**   Which overseas cricketer scored 1941 runs, including eight centuries, for the county in 1982?

22   **SIX**   Who scored three consecutive County Championship hundreds for Derbyshire in 1990?

23   **THREE**   Which Derbyshire pace bowler made his England debut versus Australia at Trent Bridge in 1989?

24   **FOUR**   Who in 1984 ended a long struggle for his maiden first-class hundred by hitting 130 against Lancashire at Old Trafford in his 380th innings?

25   **FOUR**   Which Derbyshire batsman played in all three Tests for England against India in 1990?

SINGLES (11) In 1981 Derbyshire were the first winners of the Nat West Trophy. Name their victorious side.

INNINGS SCORE:

ODDITIES

1 **FOUR** Which West Indian Test batsman of the 1980s has the christian names Hilary Angelo?

2 **FOUR** Which member of the 1991 England rugby union World Cup final side has played first-class cricket?

3 **SIX** Name the Australian left-hand batsman who was nicknamed 'The Kamikaze Kid' for running out his opening partners during the 1978–79 Ashes series.

4 **TWO** Who was Viv Richards' best man at his wedding in Antigua in March 1981?

5 **THREE** What is Fred Trueman's middle name?

6 **FOUR** Name the former detective sergeant in the Nottingham fraud squad who made his Test debut as an umpire in 1988.

7 **THREE** Who is the England batsman who scored a first-class century against Cambridge University on 13 April 1991, the earliest hundred of any English season?

8 **SIX** Which leg-spinner on the 1975 Australian tour of England was bowled by the only delivery he faced during their 15-match programme?

9 **THREE** Sussex spinner Ian Salisbury made his Test debut in 1992 against Pakistan at Lord's. In his first innings he was dismissed in unusual circumstances. How?

10 **TWO** Which British Prime Minister was voted Best Young Cricketer at the age of 12 by the London *Evening Standard*?

11 **SIX** Len Durtanovich, a Yugoslavian immigrant, has played Test cricket for Australia. By what name is he better known?

12 **FOUR** Which Kent and England all-rounder, who was banned from Test cricket for touring South Africa in 1990, made his debut for the Canterbury Amateur Operatic Society in April 1989 in a production of *Fiddler on the Roof*?

13 **THREE** Which West Indian batsman scored 214 and 100* against New Zealand on his Test debut in 1971–72, but had limited further opportunities due partly to an allergy to grass?

*Not out innings

14   **FOUR** Who is the only ordained minister to have played Test cricket?

15   **SIX** What happened just three hours after the England team arrived in India for their 1984–85 tour?

16   **THREE** Which famous umpire wrote the following books: *Not-Out, That's Out* and *From the Pavilion End*?

17   **FOUR** Why did New Zealanders Bruce Murray and Vic Pollard refuse to play against England in the 2nd Test at Auckland in 1970–71?

18   **SIX** Andrew Hilditch, the Australian vice-captain on the 1985 tour of England, is married to the daughter of which famous Australian skipper?

19   **FOUR** Which Pakistan opener was given out 'handled the ball' during their Test match against Australia at Karachi in 1982–83?

20   **THREE** Which West Indian batsman's autobiography is entitled *Hitting Across the Line*?

21   **SIX** Which Australian spin bowler was banned for life in 1981, for telling blue jokes whilst ladies were present, by the Queensland Cricketers' Club?

22   **FOUR** Which former Pakistan captain is the son of a doctor who represented India?

23   **THREE** Which Durham pace bowler, who joined them from Northamptonshire for the 1992 season, was offered a scholarship to play basketball in America?

24   **FOUR** How did pressman Vaughan Scott upset the England team during the 3rd Test at Wellington in February 1992?

25   **FOUR** An England wicket-keeper had the misfortune to suffer the following series of accidents on the 1987–88 Pakistan tour:
    a) He was hit on the head by a ball returned by a spectator
    b) As he walked across the hospital grounds to receive treatment for the cut he was knocked down by an erratic motorist
    c) He completed an unwanted hat-trick by hitting his head on a light as he rose from the stitching operation.
Who is he?

SINGLES (8) Since 1980, eight West Indian-born players have represented England in Tests. Name them.

INNINGS SCORE:

AUSTRALIA

1   **SIX**   How was Andrew Hilditch controversially dismissed in the second innings of the Perth Test against Pakistan in 1978–79?

2   **FOUR**   At the Oval on 14 August 1948, Don Bradman needed four runs in his last Test innings to attain a Test average of 100. Who bowled him second ball for a duck?

3   **FOUR**   Who, aged 19 years 121 days, scored 153 versus India at Melbourne in 1947–48?

4   **TWO**   Who scored 1219 Test runs in the calendar year commencing 1 January 1989?

5   **SIX**   For which Australian state side did Tom Graveney play?

6   **FOUR**   Who in January 1989 made his Australian Test debut aged 35, the fifth oldest Australian debutant since the war?

7   **SIX**   Which Australian Test batsman had his cheekbone fractured by a Tony Pigott delivery in a tour game at Hove in 1989?

8   **FOUR**   Which Australian bowler took a broken hat-trick against the West Indies in Perth in 1988 – only the second such occurrence in Test cricket, just two weeks after the first?

9   **SIX**   Which spin bowler took 6–78 versus England at Sydney in January 1987 on his Test debut?

10   **THREE**   Which county side were the only team to beat the 1989 touring Australians in a first-class game?

11   **TWO**   Which legendary player is the only batsman to score centuries in six successive Test matches?

12   **FOUR**   Who hit 12 sixes in an innings versus Warwickshire in 1989, the most sixes scored by an Australian?

13   **TWO**   Who was the first Australian wicket-keeper to score a century in a Test match?

14   **FOUR**   Name the Australian Test batsman who scored a hundred runs between lunch and tea at the Queen's Park Oval, Trinidad in 1973.

15 **THREE** Which famous Australian player was given the christian names of Keith and Ross after the first airman to travel from England to Australia?

16 **FOUR** Who took 11–222 against the West Indies in the 1960 Brisbane tied Test?

17 **SIX** Who was the first New South Wales bowler to take 300 Sheffield Shield wickets?

18 **FOUR** Which England batsman, whilst playing for Western Australia in the 1969 Sheffield Shield, scored 181 between lunch and tea against Queensland?

19 **SIX** Name either of the two South Australian batsmen who put on a 462-run partnership versus Tasmania in the Sheffield Shield in March 1987.

20 **SIX** Which Western Australian batsman scored 262 in the 1987 Sheffield Shield final?

21 **THREE** Which Australian left-arm pace bowler was due to join Hampshire for the 1988 season but was unable to do so owing to a serious back injury?

22 **THREE** Which Australian slow bowler took the wicket of Carl Hooper in the 2nd Test at Georgetown in 1991, his first success in 101 Test match overs?

23 **TWO** Which Australian batsman was controversially run out off a Courtney Walsh no-ball in the 2nd Test versus the West Indies in 1991?

24 **FOUR** Who scored a hundred and a double hundred in the 5th Test against the West Indies in 1968–69, to become the first batsman to do so in Test history?

25 **THREE** Which Australian, who needed an overnight stop in hospital to recover from heat exhaustion, scored 210 versus India in the 1986 tied Test in Madras?

SINGLES (19) England beat Australia 2–0 in the 1970–71 Test series Down Under. Name the 19 players used by Australia in the series.

INNINGS SCORE:

COUNTY CHAMPIONSHIP

1   **SIX**   Up to the start of the 1993 season, which county had lost the most County Championship games?

2   **FOUR**   And which county had won the most County Championship games?

3   **THREE**   Which county won seven consecutive County Championship titles between 1952 and 1958?

4   **SIX**   Which county, who last won the title when they shared it with Surrey in 1950, were unbeaten during the 1974 season but could only finish eighth?

5   **FOUR**   Which Yorkshireman made the record number of County Championship appearances, 763, from 1898 to 1930?

6   **FOUR**   Glamorgan won their second County Championship title in 1969. But which county, who have never won this honour, were 52 points clear of the Welsh county on the 13 August that year?

7   **SIX**   Which overseas cricketer hit six successive sixes off Dennis Breakwell in the Gloucestershire versus Somerset fixture in August 1979?

8   **FOUR**   Which county went 208 games with only nine defeats between 1922 and 1928?

9   **TWO**   In 1925, which county lost 20 of their 26 games in only their fifth County Championship season?

10   **FOUR**   Who took 8–44, including a hat-trick, for Warwickshire versus Derbyshire in their last Championship game of 1972 to secure the title?

11   **THREE**   Which county won their first ever Championship title in 1979?

12   **SIX**   (*Two runs each*) When Yorkshire won the 1966 County Championship, which three bowlers took over 100 wickets?

13   **FOUR**   Which company sponsored the Championship from 1977 to 1983?

14   **FOUR**   Which Northern county won their last County Championship title in 1936?

15 **FOUR** Which county's best finish in the competition is third, in 1892, 1958, 1963, 1966 and 1981?

16 **SIX** When Lancashire won the title in 1934, which famous 52-year-old batsman was the only player to score a hundred against them?

17 **FOUR** When did the Championship last end in a tie?

18 **SIX** Which county beat Gloucestershire on 12 August 1912 to win the title, the earliest ever date for securing the trophy?

19 **FOUR** Who has taken the most wickets in County Championship history?

20 **THREE** When Essex won the 1991 Britannic Assurance County Championship, who were the unfortunate runners-up who had led the Championship race since early June?

21 **TWO** Which overseas batsman, who did not return to play in England in 1992, scored the most runs in the 1991 County Championship?

22 **FOUR** Which county won the 1974 Championship by just two points?

23 **FOUR** Nottinghamshire won the Championship in 1981 for the first time in 52 years. But which team did they just pip – for what would have been their first ever title – by a mere two points?

24 **TWO** Which knighted all-rounder achieved the 'double' – 1000 runs and 100 wickets – in 1984, the first time it had been done since Fred Titmus in 1967?

25 **THREE** Who took successive County Championship winning medals in 1971 and 1972 with different counties?

SINGLES (8)   The 1890 County Championship was contested between which eight sides?

INNINGS SCORE:

7 DURHAM

1 **SIX** Who played for Durham in Minor County cricket in 1979 after representing New Zealand in the Prudential World Cup?

2 **FOUR** Where did Durham stage their first ever County Championship fixture?

3 **THREE** Which county side did Durham beat in the first round of the 1973 Gillette Cup?

4 **SIX** Which batsman hit 200 not out for Durham against Victoria in their 1991 match against the Sheffield Shield champions?

5 **FOUR** Which former Nottinghamshire reserve wicket-keeper joined Durham for the 1992 season?

6 **THREE** Who was the first Durham batsman to score 1000 first-class runs?

7 **FOUR** Which first-class county did Durham beat in the first round of the 1985 Nat West Trophy?

8 **THREE** Which former England batsman left Northamptonshire in 1990 to become Durham's director of coaching?

9 **SIX** In the 1991 Minor Counties Championship (Eastern Division), Durham could only finish in third place. Which side won that title and went on to beat Oxfordshire in the Championship final?

10 **FOUR** Which county did Durham beat in their first ever Sunday League fixture on 19 April 1992?

11 **TWO** Which former England captain joined the county for the 1992 season?

12 **FOUR** Which Durham all-rounder was named as one of Wisden's five Cricketers of the Year in 1985 whilst with Gloucestershire?

13 **SIX** Which Durham player, recruited for the 1992 campaign, played for Cambridge University (1976–78) whilst his father was the Sports Editor of ITN?

14 **FOUR** Who hit 109 for Durham versus Glamorgan at Darlington in the 1991 Nat West Trophy, the first century by a Durham player in the history of the 60-over competition?

15   **SIX**   Which Victorian and Australian pace bowler took 7–32 against Lancashire in the 1983 Nat West Trophy first round?

16   **THREE**   Which cricketer left Somerset in 1991 to become Durham's captain?

17   **FOUR**   Which batsman hit a century against Leicestershire on 29 April 1992 to become Durham's first ever County Championship centurian?

18   **FOUR**   Gary Brown appeared for Durham in 1992, but which county does his brother Keith play for?

19   **THREE**   Which Durham pace bowler represented Worcestershire between 1985 and 1990 and took 52 first-class wickets in 1989?

20   **FOUR**   Which 17-year-old all-rounder celebrated his first-class debut by taking the wickets of three former Test players (Huw Morris, Viv Richards and Matthew Maynard) for just 20 runs in 56 balls during Durham's match against Glamorgan in May 1992?

21   **TWO**   Who joined Durham for the 1992 season having already scored over 20 000 first-class runs since his debut in 1972?

22   **SIX**   Durham drew with Hampshire in the Britannic Assurance Championship on 1 June 1992. Which pace bowler, who allegedly weighs over 16 stone, took Tony Middleton's wicket with his first ball in first-class cricket?

23   **FOUR**   Which team did Durham beat by an innings and 104 runs to register their first Championship win on 16 May 1992?

24   **THREE**   Which Durham batsman scored a hundred in each innings against Pakistan in July 1992 for the second time in his career?

25   **FOUR**   Which county beat Durham in a Britannic Assurance Championship game on 6 August 1992 to win the inaugural Light Infantry Cup?

SINGLES (11) Durham faced Leicestershire in their first ever County Championship fixture commencing on 25 April 1992. Name their side.

INNINGS SCORE:

MODERN CRICKETING HEROES I

GRAHAM GOOCH

1 **FOUR** Gooch scored 333 versus India at Lord's in 1990, but who held the record for the previous highest score for England against India?

2 **THREE** Gooch's 333 was also the highest score by a Test captain. Which Australian skipper had scored 311 versus England at Old Trafford in 1964?

3 **FOUR** During that 1990 Lord's Test, Gooch scored 456 runs – the highest match aggregate in Test history. Which Australian batsman previously held the record?

4 **FOUR** In 1990 Gooch scored the most Test runs (1058) in an English summer. Which batsman previously held the record?

5 **THREE** Gooch went on to score three consecutive Test centuries in 1990. Who was the last Englishman to do this before him?

6 **SIX** Gooch scored his first Test match century in his 36th innings, but who were England's opponents?

SIR RICHARD HADLEE

7 **SIX** Which former Kent and Pakistan captain was Hadlee's first Test match victim?

8 **FOUR** For which Australian state side has Hadlee appeared?

9 **THREE** On the 1973 tour of England, Richard Hadlee only played in one Test match but one of his brothers played in all three. Name him.

10 **FOUR** Which Englishman was involved in Hadlee's last Test dismissal both as batsman and bowler?

11 **FOUR** When Hadlee received his knighthood, where did the words Sir Richard Hadlee first appear on a Test match scorecard?

12 **FOUR** On which Test match ground did Hadlee take his 400th Test wicket?

IAN BOTHAM

13 **FOUR** Which Australian Test captain was Botham's first victim in Test cricket?

14 **THREE** In 1979, when Botham took his 100th Test wicket, his victim was the Indian Test captain. Name him.

15 **SIX** In taking his 100th Test wicket, Botham became the quickest all-rounder to pass the 1000 run/100 wicket milestone in Test cricket history. Whose record did he beat?

16 **SIX** Botham had to return from England's 1983–84 tour of Pakistan with a knee injury. He had just equalled whose record of 64 consecutive Test match appearances for England?

17 **SIX** Where did Botham score his first Test century?

18 **TWO** (*One run each*) Botham's 200th and 300th Test wicket victims were both wicket-keepers. Name them.

VIV RICHARDS

19 **THREE** Where did Richards score 291 versus England in 1976?

20 **SIX** Who was Richards' first captain at Somerset?

21 **FOUR** Richards scored 132 not out to help Somerset beat whom in the 1981 Gillette Cup final?

22 **FOUR** For which Australian state side has Richards appeared?

23 **SIX** Against whom did Richards score 322 at Taunton in 1985?

24 **THREE** Where did Richards score his memorable innings of 189 in a Texaco Trophy match in 1984?

25 **FOUR** With whom did Richards share a record Somerset eighth-wicket stand of 172 at Leicester in 1983?

SINGLES (4) When Graham Gooch scored 154 not out versus the West Indies at Headingley in 1991 he became only the fifth batsman to score Test hundreds on all English Test grounds (Sheffield excepted). Name the other four.

INNINGS SCORE:

WORLD CUP 1992

1 **THREE** Which team did England dismiss for just 74 runs at Adelaide in an abandoned group game?

2 **FOUR** Who became the only cricketer to be on the losing side in three World Cup finals?

3 **FOUR** Who was the only English umpire at the tournament?

4 **THREE** When England beat Australia in Sydney, which Englishman played despite suffering from nervous colic?

5 **FOUR** Which former Warwickshire batsman was appointed an England selector during the World Cup?

6 **SIX** Who, with 285 runs, was England's top scorer during the tournament?

7 **FOUR** What do Pakistan, the 1992 winners, have in common with the previous four World Cup victors?

8 **SIX** Who was the Zimbabwean farmer who took 4–21 to lead his country to a shock win over England at Albury in their final group game?

9 **TWO** Who scored 60 off just 37 balls to earn the Man of the Match award in Pakistan's victory over New Zealand in the semi-final?

10 **FOUR** Who was named as Man of the Match in the final and was the top wicket-taker in the tournament?

11 **SIX** Name the Zimbabwean spinner who had previously played Test cricket for South Africa.

12 **THREE** Which legendary batsman, surprisingly not selected for the 1992 tournament, has scored the most runs (1113) in the history of the competition?

13 **SIX** Which England all-rounder hit 18 off the last over of their semi-final?

14 **THREE** (*One each*) Which three England players appeared in both the 1987 and 1992 World Cup finals?

15 **FOUR** Who scored 456 runs, averaging over 100, before leaving to coach in Italy?

16 **SIX** Which opener hit 119, the highest score of the 1992 World Cup, during Pakistan's defeat of New Zealand at Christchurch?

17 **TWO** Which team were set a ridiculous target of 22 off the last ball to beat England in their rain-affected semi-final?

18 **THREE** Who was England's top wicket-taker with 16 dismissals at an average of 19.12?

19 **SIX** Against which country did New Zealand amass 312–4 at New Plymouth in a group game?

20 **FOUR** Which Australian bowler, the top wicket-taker in the 1987 competition, took a wicket with the first legitimate delivery of the 1992 event?

21 **SIX** Name the West Indies' top wicket-taker in the tournament, who was controversially omitted from their Test team to face South Africa the following month.

22 **FOUR** Pakistan beat England in the 1992 final. But who beat the tournament winners by the convincing margin of 10 wickets in their first group game at Melbourne?

23 **THREE** Which 1992 skipper has now taken the most wickets (33) in the history of the competition?

24 **SIX** Which New Zealander scored 100 versus Australia in the opening game to register the first century in the 1992 tournament?

25 **TWO** Which team surprisingly won the group stages before losing in the semi-finals?

SINGLES (11) Name the victorious Pakistan side that beat England in the final at Melbourne on 25 March 1992.

INNINGS SCORE:

ESSEX

1   **THREE**   Who scored 176 for the county against Glamorgan in a Sunday League game in 1983 to create a competition batting record?

2   **FOUR**   Where would you see cricket played at Chalkwell Park?

3   **THREE**   Which former Essex spinner represented Great Britain at fencing in the 1968 and 1972 Olympics?

4   **SIX**   Graham Gooch's cousin has also played for the county. Can you name him?

5   **FOUR**   Who, on 27 July 1985, celebrated his 26th birthday by catching the first eight Somerset wickets?

6   **TWO**   Which Essex left-arm bowler was called up into the 1991 England 'A' squad on tour in Sri Lanka to replace the injured Steve Watkin?

7   **FOUR**   Which overseas player scored 1023 runs and took 82 wickets in the 1972 season?

8   **FOUR**   Who played in 301 consecutive County Championship games between May 1961 and July 1972?

9   **FOUR**   Which famous all-rounder, now a radio commentator, took his 2000th wicket in 1965 to become only the fifth player to score over 25 000 runs and take 2000 wickets in first-class cricket?

10   **FOUR**   Which former England spinner scored a century in only 44 minutes against the Australians at Chelmsford in 1975?

11   **THREE**   Which England debutant scored 1890 runs in the 1968 season?

12   **SIX**   Which all-rounder, who now resides in South Africa, achieved the 'double' on 25 July 1963, the sixth earliest this milestone has been reached?

13   **SIX**   Which batsman, who later became a Test selector, scored nine first-class hundreds in the 1955 season?

14   **THREE**   Which overseas player left the county in 1985 after scoring over 16 000 Championship runs in just 11 seasons with Essex?

15   **TWO**   Which pace bowler was named Young Cricketer of the Year in 1983?

16   **FOUR**   Which Essex batsman scored two centuries in the match for Scotland v MCC at Aberdeen in 1971?

17   **TWO**   Which Pakistan Test cricketer replaced Mark Waugh as the Essex overseas player for the 1991 and 1993 seasons?

18   **THREE**   In which country was Derek Pringle born?

19   **SIX**   Which Essex all-rounder took 754 wickets (av. 25.83) and scored 8729 runs (av. 23.15) in the County Championship between 1965 and 1986, but never represented England?

20   **FOUR**   Which England bowler took 106 first-class wickets for the county in both 1978 and 1979?

21   **SIX**   In June 1991 Essex played a special benefit match for David East. In which country was the match held?

22   **THREE**   Which former England all-rounder captained the side from 1961–66?

23   **SIX**   Which overseas cricketer took 9–61 versus Cambridge University on his debut for the county at Brentwood in 1966?

24   **FOUR**   After winning the 1991 County Championship Essex took part in a Championship Challenge game against the winners of the Sheffield Shield. Who were their opponents?

25   **FOUR**   Where would you be watching Essex play if you were spectating at Southchurch Park?

SINGLES (11) When Essex beat Surrey by 35 runs to win the 1979 Benson & Hedges Cup, it was their first honour of any kind since their inception in 1876. Can you name their victorious side?

INNINGS SCORE:

av. = average

PICTURE QUIZ 1

1   **FOUR**   Name this picturesque ground where touring sides traditionally start their fixtures in England. ▼

2   **FOUR**   Which English Test ground is featured here? ▼

INNINGS SCORE:

3 FOUR Controversial Test match umpire Shakoor Rana has just raised his finger to answer an appeal made by which famous all rounder? ▶

4a FOUR *(Two runs each)* Which two batsmen are shown leaving the field in triumph? ▼

4b FOUR What has just happened?

5 SINGLES (16) Identify each member of this England team group that toured the West Indies in 1986. ▼

11 SPINNERS

1   **THREE**   Which 34-year-old England off-spinner took the wicket of Javed Miandad with his fourth ball in Test cricket at Edgbaston in 1982?

2   **THREE**   Which England off-spinner, whose county career started back in 1949, went on to play in five decades?

3   **FOUR**   Lancashire's David Hughes hit 26 off the last over of the 1976 Gillette Cup final. Who was the unlucky bowler?

4   **SIX**   Which New Zealand spinner scored 110 at Trent Bridge in 1986 to register his maiden Test hundred?

5   **SIX**   Which famous pace bowler was 12th man when spinner Jim Laker took 19 Australian wickets at Old Trafford in 1956?

6   **FOUR**   Which England spinner took 6–79 in Australia's second innings of the 1st Test in 1968, but was dropped for the next game?

7   **FOUR**   Ian Salisbury made his Test debut for England against Pakistan in 1992. But who was the last leg-spinner before him to represent England, 21 years earlier?

8   **SIX**   Which slow left-arm bowler, who no longer plays county cricket, took 74 first-class wickets (av. 25) for Lancashire in the 1987 season?

9   **TWO**   Which famous England slow left-arm bowler scored his maiden first-class hundred against Sussex in 1985?

10   **THREE**   Justin Vaughan was given out to the bowling of Graeme Hick during the England XI v New Zealand Emerging XI game at Hamilton in January 1992. Why was his dismissal so unusual?

11   **FOUR**   Which England spinner completed the 1000 runs and 100 wicket Test double after hitting a half-century against Pakistan at the Oval in 1987?

12   **SIX**   When Phil Edmonds ricked his neck whilst driving just before the Lord's Test match against New Zealand in 1983, which slow bowler replaced him at the eleventh hour?

13   **FOUR**   Which veteran spinner went out to bat as a night-watchman for England against Australia at Sydney in 1983 and scored 95?

14 **THREE** Which England spinner took 6 wickets for just 2 runs in 51 deliveries, registering his best Test match figures (8–51), against Pakistan at Lord's in 1974?

15 **SIX** Which famous off-spinner took 8 wickets for just 2 runs in the Test trial at Bradford in 1950?

16 **FOUR** Which overseas bowler took 123 wickets at just 18 apiece for Warwickshire in 1971?

17 **THREE** Which Pakistan leg-spin and googly bowler was sent home from the 1985 tour of New Zealand for 'disciplinary reasons'?

18 **SIX** Which 38-year-old spinner had match figures of 10–144 to help Australia beat West Indies at Sydney in the final Test of their 1984–85 series?

19 **SIX** Which England off-spinner took 4 wickets in 5 balls versus New Zealand at Headingley in 1965?

20 **SIX** Which New Zealand off-spinner became only the second cricketer to take a hat-trick on his Test debut when he dismissed Javed Miandad, Wasim Raja and Intikhab Alam at Lahore in 1976?

21 **FOUR** Which famous spin bowler, who was the first East Indian to represent the West Indies, took 26 Test wickets (av. 23.23) on their 1950 tour of England?

22 **TWO** Which former Australian captain, who has remained a household name through his work as a cricket journalist and broadcaster, was a Public Relations Officer for Kerry Packer's World Series Cricket?

23 **THREE** For which county did Shaun Udal play in the 1992 Benson & Hedges Cup final?

24 **FOUR** Name the Somerset off-break bowler who took their first hat-trick for ten years at Gloucester in May 1992.

25 **THREE** Which England left-arm spinner took 5–17 off just 65 balls on his Test debut versus Australia at Leeds in 1975?

SINGLES (7) Which seven spin bowlers have taken 200 or more Test match wickets?

INNINGS SCORE:

ASHES TESTS I

1 **SIX** When Ian Botham took the wicket of Jeff Thomson at the end of the 4th Test at Melbourne in 1982, he became only the second Englishman to take 100 wickets and score 1000 runs in Ashes Tests. Who was the first?

2 **FOUR** Which Englishman was named Man of the Match in the 1977 Centenary Test at Melbourne?

3 **FOUR** Which Australian bowler was rejected by Northamptonshire in 1970, but only two years later took 16 wickets in a Lord's Test?

4 **SIX** Which Australian scored a century in the famous Headingley Test of 1981?

5 **THREE** Which ground staged England's first home Test match against Australia?

6 **SIX** When Ian Botham was selected for the 1st Test against Australia in 1989, he had to pull out of the squad after a triple fracture of the cheekbone. Which Glamorgan bowler caused the injury?

7 **FOUR** Who scored 188 versus Australia at Melbourne in 1975, the highest score by a touring skipper in a Test match in Australia?

8 **FOUR** Which pace bowler took 22 wickets for Australia in the 1982–83 Ashes series?

9 **THREE** Who caught Bob Woolmer at Trent Bridge in 1981 to become the first wicket-keeper to make 100 dismissals in Ashes Tests?

10 **SIX** At Melbourne in 1982–83, England beat Australia by just 3 runs to equal the record for the narrowest winning margin in Tests. But who caught Jeff Thomson after Chris Tavare had knocked up a slip chance?

11 **TWO** On which ground did Australia stage their first Ashes Test?

12 **FOUR** Which famous Australian skipper was known as 'The Big Ship'?

13 **FOUR** Who was Douglas Jardine's vice-captain on the infamous 'Bodyline Tour' in 1932–33?

14 **SIX** Which England batsman was hit on the head by a Lindwall bouncer in the Old Trafford Test of 1948, but returned to score 145 not out?

15 **FOUR** Who put on 451 with Don Bradman on the first day of the 1934 Oval Test?

16 **FOUR** In the 3rd Test at Birmingham in 1989, Steve Waugh was bowled for 43 – his first dismissal of the series after amassing 593 runs. Which Englishman, who was making his debut, finally captured his wicket?

17 **SIX** The 1975 Headingley Test was abandoned because of pitch vandalism. Can you name the convict whose release the vandals demanded?

18 **FOUR** Who scored 175 for England in the 2nd Test at Lord's in 1975, his seventh hundred against Australia?

19 **TWO** Who, at Melbourne in 1954–55, scored 102 out of England's total of 191, to equal the record for the lowest Ashes Test innings total to contain a century?

20 **THREE** Which Australian bowler had match figures of 11–165 in the 1977 Centenary Test?

21 **FOUR** Who was the only Englishman to play in both Centenary Tests, at Melbourne (1977) and Lord's (1980)?

22 **THREE** Which controversial English bowler took match figures of 8–63 in the 4th Test at Sydney in 1970–71?

23 **FOUR** Which England swing bowler had match figures of 10–104 in the 5th Test at the Oval in 1985?

24 **TWO** Who captained Australia in the Headingley Test of 1981?

25 **FOUR** Which Australian, batting at number ten, scored 74 in the 2nd Test at Lord's in 1989?

SINGLES (10) Jim Laker took 19 wickets in the Old Trafford Test in 1956. Name the rest of the England side.

INNINGS SCORE:

13   INDIA

1   **FOUR**   When England lost a series against India for the first time in 1961–62, who was the unfortunate England captain?

2   **SIX**   Which Indian batsman struck 6 fours off a Bob Willis over in the 2nd Test at Old Trafford in 1982?

3   **FOUR**   Which prolific batsman scored two centuries in the 3rd Test against the West Indies at Calcutta in 1978–79?

4   **THREE**   Who was named Man of the Match in the 1983 World Cup final?

5   **FOUR**   When England scored 633–5 declared against India in the 1st Test at Edgbaston in 1979, which Indian all-rounder took all five wickets to fall?

6   **THREE**   For which English county did Sunil Gavaskar appear?

7   **FOUR**   Why did Bishen Bedi declare India's second innings of the last Test at Kingston in 1976 with only five wickets down?

8   **THREE**   Who captained India to victory in the 1983 World Cup final?

9   **FOUR**   Where did India score 42 all out in the 2nd Test of the 1974 series against England?

10   **FOUR**   When Graham Gooch scored his magnificent innings of 333 at Lord's in 1990, which Indian bowler finally took his wicket?

11   **FOUR**   Which Indian spinner took 35 wickets in the 1971 Test series against England?

12   **SIX**   Which all-rounder batted on all five days of the Calcutta Test against England in 1985–86?

13   **SIX**   Which batsman hit 126 not out at Lord's in 1986 to register his third hundred in three Tests there?

14   **SIX**   Who scored 189 not out against England in the New Delhi Test of the 1961–62 series?

15   **FOUR**   Where did India astonish the cricket world by scoring 403–4 to beat the West Indies in 1976?

16   **SIX**   Where did India play their first ever Test match?

17   **SIX**   Who took seven catches against England at Bangalore in 1976–77 to equal the record for catches by an outfielder in a Test match?

18   **FOUR**   For which Indian team did Lancashire wicket-keeper Farokh Engineer play for?

19   **FOUR**   Who, aged just 18 years 214 days, made his Test debut for India versus Australia at Madras in 1969–70?

20   **FOUR**   Who bowled 59 consecutive overs for India against England at the Oval in 1990?

21   **FOUR**   Who, at Lord's in 1990, scored a Test century off just 87 balls in 130 minutes?

22   **SIX**   Which Test batsman, who hit over 6000 Test runs for India, married Sunil Gavaskar's sister?

23   **TWO**   Which left-arm spinner took 266 wickets for his country in just 67 Tests?

24   **SIX**   Who took 9–102 for India versus the West Indies at Kanpur in 1958–59?

25   **FOUR**   For which county did Srinivasaraghavan Venkataraghavan (usually abbreviated to Venkat!) play in the 1970s?

SINGLES (11) Name the Indian side that tied with Australia at Madras in 1986.

INNINGS SCORE:

GLAMORGAN

1   **TWO**   Which left-handed batsman scored ten centuries for Glamorgan in 1990?

2   **FOUR**   Which West Indian cricketer took a hat-trick for the county against Kent in the Benson & Hedges Cup at Cardiff in 1981?

3   **THREE**   Which famous Test batsman scored three successive hundreds ɪor Glamorgan in 1990?

4   **FOUR**   Which Pakistan batsman hit 147 for Glamorgan before lunch versus the West Indians at Swansea in 1969?

5   **SIX**   Which overseas bowler took 9–49 for Glamorgan versus Leicestershire at Colwyn Bay in their 1969 Championship-winning season?

6   **THREE**   Which former England skipper, now better known as a television commentator and journalist, led the county from 1967 to 1972?

7   **SIX**   Who scored 230 for Glamorgan versus Worcestershire at Worcester in 1977, to register the fourth highest score for the county?

8   **TWO**   Javed Miandad joined Glamorgan in 1980, but for which county had he previously played?

9   **THREE**   Name the opening batsman who scored 34056 first-class runs for the county between 1957 and 1983, a Glamorgan record.

10   **SIX**   Which Glamorgan cricketer, ironically dismissed in 1965 at Lord's for handling the ball, was capped three times for Wales at rugby union before switching codes to play rugby league for Leeds?

11   **THREE**   Which BBC Wales commentator took 101 wickets, scored 1347 runs and took 73 catches in the 1961 season?

12   **FOUR**   Who was the first Glamorgan bowler to take 2000 first-class wickets?

13   **THREE**   When Glamorgan entertained the touring Australians in 1985 they played at 'The Gnoll' for the first time in 11 years. Where is 'The Gnoll'?

14   **FOUR**   Which left-arm bowler took 9–56 in a County Championship game against Hampshire at Basingstoke in 1975?

15   **THREE**   Which West Indian batsman put on 330 with Alan Jones for the first wicket against Northamptonshire at Swansea in 1972?

16   **TWO**   Which recent England Test opener captained Glamorgan from 1986 to 1989, but relinquished the role to concentrate on his batting?

17   **FOUR**   Colin Metson joined Glamorgan in 1987, but for which county had he previously kept wicket?

18   **FOUR**   Which former England Test cricketer scored two double hundreds for Glamorgan in the 1991 County Championship?

19   **TWO**   Which famous Glamorgan batsman played in one match for England against the Rest of the World in 1970?

20   **SIX**   Name the West Indian all-rounder who appeared for the county in 1990.

21   **FOUR**   Who scored 102 out of 117, reaching his century with three successive sixes, in just 87 minutes versus Yorkshire on his first-class debut at Swansea in 1985?

22   **THREE**   Who was the unfortunate bowler hit for six successive sixes by Gary Sobers at Swansea in 1968?

23   **TWO**   Who scored 313 not out for Somerset versus Glamorgan at Cardiff in 1990, a record score against the county?

24   **SIX**   Who was the former England leg-spin bowler who put on 140 with Rodney Ontong for the tenth wicket versus Hampshire at Swansea in 1981?

25   **THREE**   In which city do Glamorgan play at Sophia Gardens?

SINGLES (12) As at 1 April 1993, twelve players have represented England whilst playing for Glamorgan. Name them.

INNINGS SCORE:

DOMESTIC ONE-DAY CRICKET

1   **FOUR**   Sussex beat Worcestershire to win the first Gillette Cup final. But which Worcestershire and England slow bowler took the Man of the Match award?

2   **FOUR**   Which overseas batsman scored 1116 runs (av. 50.72) for Essex in all forms of one-day cricket in 1980?

3   **FOUR**   David Hughes hit 24 off an over for Lancashire versus Gloucestershire in a memorable Gillette Cup semi-final in 1972. But who was the unfortunate bowler?

4   **TWO**   What was significant about Hertfordshire's defeat of Derbyshire in the 1991 Nat West Trophy second round?

5   **THREE**   Which England batsman scored 146 in the 1965 Gillette Cup final on a pitch both sets of captains had deemed unfit for play?

6   **FOUR**   Which Scottish-born cricketer was named Man of the Match in the 1985 Nat West Trophy final between Essex and Nottinghamshire?

7   **THREE**   Which county won the 1988 Benson & Hedges Cup final on their first visit to Lord's for a one-day final?

8   **FOUR**   Which county lost the 1981 Nat West Trophy final to Derbyshire and the 1987 Benson & Hedges Cup final to Yorkshire both with the scores tied?

9   **SIX**   For which team did John O'Brien take a hat-trick in the 1988 Nat West Trophy competition?

10   **THREE**   Lancashire were the first county to win five September one-day finals – but who was the only player to appear in all five?

11   **SIX**   Which team scored just 39 versus Sussex in a Nat West Trophy game at Hove in 1985?

12   **FOUR**   Which former Australian Test bowler took 7–22 for Middlesex versus Hampshire at Lord's in the 1982 Benson & Hedges Cup competition?

13   **FOUR**   Which former Australian Test bowler took the first hat-trick in the history of the Benson & Hedges Cup competition for Leicestershire against Worcestershire in 1972?

14   **SIX**   Which was the first county to win consecutive Benson & Hedges Cup finals?

15   **SIX**   Which Somerset cricketer in 1990 scored the fastest hundreds in the history of the Sunday League and the Nat West Trophy?

16   **TWO**   Which county won both the Nat West Trophy and the Benson & Hedges Cup in 1990?

17   **FOUR**   Which Lancashire player scored an unbeaten hundred in the 1990 Sunday League on his 21st birthday?

18   **SIX**   Who was the first wicket-keeper to claim 100 victims in the Benson & Hedges Cup?

19   **THREE**   Name the captain of Somerset who in 1979 declared at 1–0 to ensure they qualified for the later stages of the Benson & Hedges Cup.

20   **FOUR**   Who were the first Minor County side to beat a first-class county in the Gillette/Nat West Trophy?

21   **FOUR**   Which Lancastrian took his 300th Sunday League wicket when he dismissed Kent's Neil Taylor in June 1989?

22   **FOUR**   Which Northamptonshire opener won the Man of the Match award in the 1992 Nat West final?

23   **FOUR**   Which West Indian bowler took 51 wickets (av. 13.72) for Middlesex in all forms of one-day cricket in 1980?

24   **SIX**   Who, at Yeovil in July 1969, had a bowling analysis of 0–0 in 8 overs for Somerset against Essex in the John Player League?

25   **THREE**   Who skippered Yorkshire when they won the 1983 John Player League?

SINGLES (7)   Up to and including 1992, seven centuries have been scored in Lord's one-day finals. Name the six different batsmen who have achieved this feat.

INNINGS SCORE:

16 BOWLERS I

1 **SIX** Which Australian spinner was the first bowler to take 200 Test match wickets?

2 **THREE** Who in 1963 took over 100 first-class wickets aged just 17?

3 **SIX** Which player normally more famous for his spin bowling, became only the second England batsman to get successive pairs during the 1984 West Indies series?

4 **THREE** Which West Indian bowler took the most first-class wickets in the 1992 season?

5 **FOUR** Which Australian pace bowler took 8–29 against the Rest of the World XI in 1971?

6 **THREE** Which spin bowler took the wicket of Richard Harden on 27 June 1992 to became only the ninth bowler to capture 1000 wickets whilst playing for Middlesex?

7 **THREE** Which former Indian Test captain was occasional-bowler Mike Atherton's first Test wicket?

8 **TWO** Which Worcestershire spinner, who made his Test debut in 1991, took 75 first-class wickets in 1990, the most that season by a spin bowler?

9 **THREE** Who bowled 774 balls, a Test record, for the West Indies in the 1st Test versus England in 1957?

10 **SIX** Garfield Harrison took 9–113, the best innings analysis of the 1990 season, playing for which side?

11 **FOUR** Which off-break bowler, more commonly known for bowling seamers, took 13–156 for England versus the West Indies at Port of Spain in 1974?

12 **THREE** Name the Sussex pace bowler who took 126 wickets in the 1966 season.

13 **SIX** Who was the last bowler to take 200 first-class wickets in an English season?

14 **FOUR** Which bowler took 100 wickets in every season between 1949 and 1968?

15   **SIX**   Which seldom-used bowler had match figures of 11–96 for Australia versus the West Indies at Sydney in the 4th Test in 1989?

16   **SIX**   When England played the West Indies in Port of Spain in 1974, they played three recognised spinners: Derek Underwood, Pat Pocock and which recent first-class umpire?

17   **FOUR**   Jim Laker played for Surrey from 1946 to 1959, but for which other county did he appear in 1962 after coming out of retirement?

18   **THREE**   Which English bowler took 27 wickets in the 1977 Ashes series?

19   **FOUR**   Who was the first Englishman to take eight West Indian wickets in a Test innings?

20   **SIX**   Which Australian bowled 40 consecutive overs in the Madras tied Test?

21   **SIX**   Who was recruited from Yorkshire League club Pudsey to play for New Zealand in the 1990 one-day internationals?

22   **TWO**   Which Pakistan spin bowler took 9–56 in an innings and the wicket of every Englishman during the Lahore Test of 1987?

23   **FOUR**   Who was Harold Larwood's regular opening new-ball partner on the Bodyline tour of Australia?

24   **FOUR**   Which all-rounder replaced the injured Ricardo Ellcock on England's 1990 tour of the West Indies?

25   **SIX**   Richard Illingworth took a wicket with his first ball in Test cricket during the 3rd Test against the West Indies at Trent Bridge in 1991. But who was the batsman he dismissed?

SINGLES (19) When England lost the 1989 Ashes series, they used an amazing 19 different bowlers. Name them.

INNINGS SCORE:

17 GLOUCESTERSHIRE

1 **THREE** Which famous Gloucestershire and England batsman scored 318 not out for the county against Yorkshire at Cheltenham back in 1876?

2 **THREE** Which Gloucestershire and England bowler attended a trial for the London Monarchs American Football team before the start of the World League?

3 **FOUR** Who in 1966 took seven catches in an innings for Gloucestershire against Nottinghamshire at Trent Bridge, a record for an outfielder?

4 **THREE** Where would you be watching cricket if you were spectating at the Winget ground, previously known as the Wagon Works?

5 **SIX** Name the England off-spinner who did the double in 1961, just one year after winning the Young Cricketer of the Year award.

6 **FOUR** Which all-rounder took a hat-trick for the county against Hampshire at Southampton in the 1977 Benson & Hedges Cup?

7 **FOUR** Who was the former Arsenal, Bristol City and England footballer who became one of the few double internationals when he made his Test debut versus New Zealand at Leeds in 1958?

8 **SIX** Jeremy Lloyds played for Gloucestershire from 1985 to 1991. For which county had he previously appeared?

9 **TWO** Which West Indian pace bowler took 118 first-class wickets in 1986?

10 **FOUR** Who replaced Bill Athey as Gloucestershire skipper in 1990?

11 **FOUR** Can you name the Zimbabwean all-rounder who played for Gloucestershire between 1985 and 1990?

12 **FOUR** Which former Gloucestershire batsman made 14 appearances for the England rugby union side between 1975 and 1979?

13 **THREE** Which famous England batsman scored 33664 runs for the county between 1920 and 1951?

14   **FOUR**   Which former England spinner completed the double in the 1959, 1963 and 1964 seasons?

15   **FOUR**   Which Pakistan Test cricketer scored centuries in four consecutive innings in 1976?

16   **SIX**   Who scored 10 672 runs for the county between 1965 and 1979 and is now a first-class umpire?

17   **FOUR**   Which overseas all-rounder took 108 wickets (av. 15.02) in the 1969 season?

18   **SIX**   Which left-handed opening batsman scored a century before lunch for Gloucestershire at The Parks on the first day of the 1980 season?

19   **SIX**   Who was the West Indian Test all-rounder who joined the county from Kent in 1982?

20   **TWO**   Can you name the wicket-keeper who made his debut against the touring Sri Lankans in 1981 and claimed eight dismissals?

21   **THREE**   From which county did Bill Athey join Gloucestershire?

22   **THREE**   Which left-arm spinner, who has since found fame with a new county, took 9–56 versus Somerset at Bristol in 1981?

23   **FOUR**   Where will you find the Pheonix County Ground?

24   **FOUR**   David Gilbert played for Gloucestershire in 1991 as the overseas replacement for Courtney Walsh. Which country has he represented?

25   **SIX**   What is 'Jack' Russell's first name?

SINGLES (11) When Gloucestershire won the 1973 Gillette Cup beating Sussex by 40 runs, it was their first major cricketing honour. Name their side.

INNINGS SCORE:

18 DEBUTS

1   **FOUR**   Which famous England cricketer, later knighted for his services to the game, scored 0 and 1 on his Test debut versus New Zealand at Lord's in 1937?

2   **THREE**   Which Yorkshireman scored 107 on his Test debut versus the West Indies at Lord's in 1969?

3   **FOUR**   On 16 December 1989 Australia played host to Sri Lanka in the first Test match ever staged at the Bellerive Oval. Where is this new Test venue?

4   **SIX**   Which Dominican-born cricketer shared in a tenth-wicket stand of 132 with Alan Hill at Sheffield in 1986 on his Derbyshire debut?

5   **SIX**   Who took 7–49 and 4–96 for England on his Test debut versus India at Lord's in 1946?

6   **THREE**   Who in 1987 made his England debut against Pakistan in the 1st Test at Old Trafford – his home ground – and was bowled for a duck off his fourth ball?

7   **TWO**   How many runs did Graham Gooch make on his Test match debut?

8   **SIX**   Which Leicestershire batsman and professional footballer made his England debut versus the West Indies at Leeds in 1976 and bagged a pair in the next Test?

9   **FOUR**   Which famous all-rounder made his international debut versus the West Indies at Scarborough in 1976?

10   **SIX**   Who is the only batsman to score a century on his debut for two different counties?

11   **THREE**   Which young Australian batsman made his Test debut versus the West Indies at Brisbane in November 1992?

12   **SIX**   Which West Indian-born cricketer made his international debut, for England, *against* the West Indies in the one-day internationals that preceded the 1988 Test series?

13   **THREE**   Which batsman and athletic fielder made his England debut versus the West Indies at Headingley in 1991?

14 **FOUR** Who was the South African bowler, engaged by Middlesex for one season only, who helped them to win the 1980 County Championship?

15 **SIX** Who was the first black player to represent a South African side? (He later played for Scotland)

16 **FOUR** Who made his debut for the West Indies in the 5th Test at the Oval in 1991?

17 **FOUR** In which year did Graeme Hick make his international debut?

18 **TWO** When Ian Botham made his Worcestershire debut in 1987, which other England cricketer also made his first appearance for the county?

19 **FOUR** Which Yorkshireman scored 74 for England on his Test debut against New Zealand at Lord's in 1987, but was dismissed four times by Richard Hadlee in the series?

20 **FOUR** Which current county cricketer made his Pakistan Test debut versus New Zealand in 1985, aged just 18?

21 **FOUR** Which England captain won five out of six tosses in his first series as skipper on the 1981–82 Indian tour?

22 **FOUR** Which spinner made his England Test debut aged 36 in the 3rd Test versus the West Indies in 1988?

23 **SIX** Name the Australian who scored 155 versus England on his Test debut at Brisbane in December 1965.

24 **THREE** Which left-handed New Zealand batsman scored 107 not out on his Test debut versus England at Auckland in 1988?

25 **FOUR** Which former Hampshire and Surrey cricketer made his Lancashire debut in 1988?

SINGLES (9) Which nine current players, as at 1 January 1993, have made just one Test appearance for England?

INNINGS SCORE:

COMEBACKS

1   **THREE**   Which famous wicket-keeper returned to the Kent side when Alan Knott was picked for England in 1967?

2   **THREE**   Which England batsman was recalled in 1976, aged 45, to face the West Indian pace attack?

3   **TWO**   Name the BBC cricket correspondent who made a comeback for Leicestershire against Essex in the 1992 Nat West Trophy semi-final.

4   **FOUR**   Which Surrey and England bowler returned to the Test match arena against the West Indies in 1984, aged 37, eight years after his last appearance?

5   **SIX**   Which former Surrey, Worcestershire and Glamorgan batsman was recalled by Pakistan in February 1987, 104 Tests after his last appearance in November 1969?

6   **FOUR**   Which England pace bowler made his comeback for Leicestershire in 1986, aged 49, and promptly took 5–22 against Yorkshire?

7   **THREE**   Which former Test spinner was recalled by Middlesex for a County Championship game at Trent Bridge in June 1992, replacing the hospitalised Phil Tufnell?

8   **FOUR**   Who in 1977–78 accepted an invitation from the Australian selectors to captain his country again after World Series cricket had claimed most of the Australian side?

9   **THREE**   Which wicket-keeper was recruited from a rum distillery in March 1990 to keep wicket for England in the West Indies?

10   **SIX**   Which county won just three of their first 17 matches in the 1965 County Championship, but recovered to win 10 of their last 11 and pip Northamptonshire for the title?

11   **FOUR**   When England wicket-keeper Bruce French was injured during the Lord's Test versus New Zealand in 1986, which former Test player returned to deputise, taking leave from his public relations work for the Test sponsors?

12   **SIX**   Who, aged 39, was recalled by the England selectors in 1966 to face the West Indies fast bowlers Hall and Griffith – and promptly hit 96?

13   **SIX**   Which Australian spinner left the game in 1977 to become a journalist, but returned in 1979–80 to play Tests against West Indies and England?

14   **FOUR**   Which veteran England batsman was flown out as an emergency replacement to face Lillee and Thomson in 1974–75?

15   **FOUR**   Which left-arm bowler was recalled by England to face India at Headingley in 1986 and took six wickets in the match?

16   **SIX**   Who in 1985 played for injury-hit Kent against the touring Australians, nine years after retiring from county cricket?

17   **THREE**   On 21 August 1992, Yorkshire returned to play Championship cricket at which venue for the first time since 1985?

18   **SIX**   Which cricketer returned to play for England against New Zealand at Lord's in 1986, his 26th Test appearance, but ruled himself out of the 1986–87 Ashes series to give his troublesome knees a rest?

19   **FOUR**   Which England batsman played against Pakistan in 1954, but was picked as first-choice wicket-keeper ten years later after only starting to wear the gloves for Sussex in 1959?

20   **FOUR**   Which famous England spinner was recalled for the 4th Test at Port of Spain in 1967–68 when in his 39th year?

21   **THREE**   Which bespectacled former England captain returned to the Test side to face Australia in 1972, after retiring back in 1967?

22   **THREE**   Which batsman, banned from Test cricket for three years for travelling to South Africa in 1982, was recalled to the England side in 1986 but pulled out injured?

23   **FOUR**   Which former England batsman returned to Northamptonshire in 1982 to play mainly as a left-arm spinner?

24   **TWO**   In the 1961 Old Trafford Test, England looked set to win, needing little more than 100 with nine wickets left. But which famous spinner took 6–70 to stage a remarkable Australian fightback?

25   **TWO**   Who in 1982, aged 50, became Yorkshire's oldest ever captain, 14 years after last playing for the white rose county?

SINGLES (11) England won the 1981 Headingley Test against Australia by 18 runs after following on. Name the side that staged this memorable fightback.

INNINGS SCORE:

HAMPSHIRE

1   **FOUR**   Which former England bowler took 9–25 for Hampshire versus Lancashire at Old Trafford in 1965, to record the best innings analysis for the county?

2   **FOUR**   Which young wicket-keeper held 10 catches in the match against Derbyshire at Portsmouth in 1981?

3   **FOUR**   Who took 2669 wickets for the county between 1948 and 1969?

4   **THREE**   Which current Hampshire player was born in Osnabruck, Germany?

5   **FOUR**   Who scored 48892 runs for the county between 1905 and 1936?

6   **THREE**   Which overseas batsman hit 13 sixes in an innings for Hampshire versus Sussex at Southampton in 1975?

7   **THREE**   Which recent Hampshire batsman, known as 'Kippy', left the county during the 1991 season to take up a marketing role in Australian cricket?

8   **SIX**   Which West Indian batsman scored 35725 runs for the county between 1945 and 1972?

9   **FOUR**   Which overseas player took 5–13 and won the Man of the Match award when Hampshire beat Derbyshire to win the 1988 Benson & Hedges Cup?

10   **THREE**   Which overseas batsman scored 2395 runs in 1968 in his first full season with the county?

11   **TWO**   Which West Indian pace bowler took 119 wickets in 1974?

12   **SIX**   When Hampshire beat Surrey to win the 1991 Nat West Trophy final, who was named Man of the Match?

13   **THREE**   Who scored 177 for Hampshire against Glamorgan in the Gillette Cup at Southampton in 1973?

14   **SIX**   Which slow bowler took 107 wickets in 1971, taking 60 wickets in the last eight matches, to miss the double by just 41 runs?

15 **SIX** Which wicket-keeper dismissed 80 batsmen for Hampshire in 1970?

16 **SIX** Who captained Hampshire to their first County Championship title in 1961?

17 **THREE** Which current Hampshire player has an Aunt Shirley who was the first lady bus driver in Barbados?

18 **FOUR** Which former Oxford University captain took over the captaincy of Hampshire in 1971?

19 **FOUR** Who in 1962, took 172 wickets off 10 303 deliveries? (Only four bowlers had ever delivered more)

20 **FOUR** Who skippered Hampshire to victory in the 1991 Nat West Trophy final?

21 **SIX** At which Test ground did Hampshire score 50 all out in 1991, to record the lowest score in the 20 year history of the Benson & Hedges Cup?

22 **FOUR** Name the Pakistan Test bowler who joined the county in 1991.

23 **TWO** Which Hampshire cricketer led the England 'B' side that toured Zimbabwe in 1989–90?

24 **FOUR** Which player represented Holland in the 1986 and 1990 ICC Trophy competitions and spends his winters as a ski instructor in the Swiss Alps?

25 **TWO** Which overseas bowler took 134 wickets in 1982?

SINGLES (13) Hampshire won the 1973 County Championship. Name the 13 players who played that season.

INNINGS SCORE:

PICTURE QUIZ 2

1   **FOUR**   Name this unique county ground. ▶

2   **FOUR**   Which English Test ground is featured here? ▼

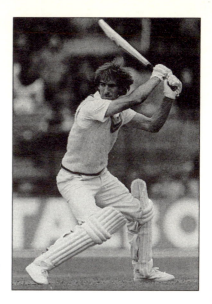

3   **FOUR**   Can you name the former England batsman pictured in his younger days? ▶

4a   **TWO**   Where was this famous Test match held? ▼

4b   **FOUR**   What happened next?

4c   **TWO**   Who was named Man of the Match?

5   **SINGLES** (14) Name this England party that represented their country in Holland in 1989. ▼

INNINGS SCORE:

ENGLISH TEST CRICKET I

1 **THREE** Which Middlesex bowler made his Test debut for England in the 3rd Test against India in 1990 after Chris Lewis had dropped out ill?

2 **SIX** Who was the only player to appear in England's last Test of the seventies and their last Test of the eighties?

3 **FOUR** Which England batsman went from July 1962 to April 1968 (78 matches) without scoring a duck in Test cricket?

4 **SIX** Which England Test bowler played for the Prime Minister's XI against his own team-mates in Rawalpindi in 1987?

5 **THREE** Name the umpire whom England skipper Mike Gatting famously confronted during the 2nd Test at Faisalabad in 1987.

6 **FOUR** Which England batsman, appearing in the 3rd Test versus Australia in 1989, was making his first appearance since playing against Sri Lanka in 1984?

7 **THREE** Name the England batsman who was the first player to reach 4000 and 5000 Test match runs.

8 **FOUR** Which fast bowler took 7–145 for England in his last Test match versus South Africa at the Oval in 1965?

9 **THREE** Who took a hat-trick for England versus the West Indies in the 4th Test at Headingley in 1957?

10 **SIX** Which Yorkshire bowler took 7–36 for England at Cape Town in the 1956–57 Test series in South Africa?

11 **FOUR** Who was the first batsman to score 7000 Test runs?

12 **FOUR** Which England batsman scored 100* versus Australia in 1985, 183* versus India in 1986 and 124 versus Pakistan in 1987 to notch up three successive Test hundreds at Edgbaston?

13 **SIX** Which Middlesex batsman scored 158 for England against New Zealand at Auckland in 1978 and came within a minute of Peter Richardson's 488-minute slowest Test century for England?

14 **FOUR** Which Lancastrian pace bowler, batting at number nine, scored 88 not out for England versus India at Old Trafford in 1971?

15 **FOUR** Which left-arm bowler made his England debut against India at New Delhi in 1976, scoring 53 and taking 10 wickets, but was accused of doctoring the ball with vaseline?

16 **FOUR** Which English bowler took 4 wickets in 5 balls at Edgbaston in the 1st Test against Pakistan in 1978?

17 **SIX** Which Northamptonshire batsman made his England debut in Sri Lanka's first ever Test match at Colombo in 1982?

18 **SIX** How many wickets did England's Johnny Briggs take against South Africa at Cape Town on 26 March 1889?

19 **THREE** Which country did England play for the first time at Lord's in 1932?

20 **THREE** Which all-rounder scored a double century for England against India in July 1982 off only 220 balls?

21 **TWO** Which English opener batted on all five days of the England-Australia Test match at Trent Bridge in 1977?

22 **THREE** Who hit 57 boundaries during his 310 not out for England versus New Zealand at Headingley in 1965?

23 **THREE** Seven venues have been used by England for home Test matches; Six are regular venues but which ground has been used just once?

24 **THREE** Who made his England Test debut at Nottingham in 1899 and his last appearance at Kingston, Jamaica in 1930?

25 **SIX** Who was aged 45 years 245 days when he captained England in the 4th Test against the West Indies at Kingston in 1948?

SINGLES (16) England's proposed tour of India in 1988–89 was cancelled for political reasons. Name the England party that was originally selected.

INNINGS SCORE:

22

NEW ZEALAND

1   **THREE**   When Sri Lanka played their first Test series against New Zealand in 1982–83, which famous New Zealand cricketer made his return to the Test arena?

2   **FOUR**   Which New Zealander was hit by a Peter Lever bouncer in the 1st Test of 1974–75 and needed heart massage at the wicket?

3   **FOUR**   Which swing bowler took 7–74 for New Zealand against England at Leeds in 1983?

4   **SIX**   Which wicket-keeper in 1990 became the first Maori to play Test cricket?

5   **FOUR**   When New Zealand won at Headingley in 1983, who was their captain?

6   **SIX**   When New Zealand beat the West Indies at Christchurch in their 1979–80 series, which West Indian bowler was reprimanded for barging into an umpire?

7   **SIX**   In which city is Test cricket played at McLean Park?

8   **FOUR·**   Where is the Basin Reserve Test ground?

9   **SIX**   Who was the New Zealand captain when they beat England for the first time at Wellington in 1978?

10   **THREE**   Which opener in 1975–76 became the only player to score 1000 runs in a New Zealand season?

11   **SIX**   Who hit 15 sixes in his innings of 296 for Wellington against Northern Districts in 1963?

12   **FOUR**   Which New Zealand Test cricketer was a team-mate of Glenn Turner's at Worcestershire?

13   **SIX**   Which New Zealand batsman hit 317 in just over four hours against a Brian Close XI at Scarborough in 1986?

14   **THREE**   (*One run each*) Martin Crowe hit his eighth Test hundred in 1988, the highest number of centuries by a New Zealand batsman. Which three retired batsmen had hit seven tons?

15 **SIX** With which state side did England tie at New Plymouth in 1978?

16 **FOUR** New Zealand won their first Test match at Auckland in 1955–56, but who were the losing side?

17 **FOUR** What is the principal cricket competition in New Zealand?

18 **FOUR** For which county did Danny Morrison appear in 1992?

19 **FOUR** Where is Lancaster Park cricket ground?

20 **TWO** Which New Zealander scored 109 versus Lancashire at Southport in 1979 to become the first batsman to score centuries against all the other 16 counties?

21 **FOUR** Who overtook Bev Congdon's Test run aggregate record (3448) for New Zealand in November 1988?

22 **FOUR** Andrew Jones and Martin Crowe put on a Test record third-wicket stand of 467 at Wellington in February 1991, but who were New Zealand's opponents?

23 **SIX** Who on 19 April 1987 took the wicket of Sri Lankan Don Anurasiri to become only the sixth New Zealander to take 100 Test wickets?

24 **SIX** Who, batting at number eleven, scored 68 not out for New Zealand versus Pakistan at Auckland in 1972–73?

25 **TWO** For which county has Martin Crowe appeared?

SINGLES (14) Prior to 1993, fourteen New Zealanders have captained their country against England in Test matches. Name them.

INNINGS SCORE:

23

ALL-ROUNDERS I

1   **TWO**   Which all-rounder took the first hat-trick in four years by a Lancashire bowler against Warwickshire on 18 August 1992?

2   **FOUR**   Which former Gloucestershire player hit five consecutive sixes in one over off Ashley Mallett for Western Province against the Australians at Cape Town in 1970?

3   **SIX**   (*Two each*) Only three Englishmen scored 500 runs and took 50 wickets in the 1991 Championship season. Name them.

4   **FOUR**   Which Test all-rounder was banned from bowling by umpire Nigel Plews during Lancashire's 1991 County Championship match against Warwickshire?

5   **FOUR**   Who is the only all-rounder to score a century and take a hat-trick in the same match *twice*?

6   **THREE**   Which Yorkshireman is the youngest player to complete the double in an English season?

7   **THREE**   For which county has Australian all-rounder Tony Dodemaide appeared?

8   **THREE**   Which famous lady cricketer, who also represented her country at hockey, captained England from 1966 to 1977 and never lost a Test match?

9   **FOUR**   Who in 1982 made his debut for England versus India, forfeiting the chance to skipper Cambridge in the Varsity match?

10   **FOUR**   For which county has South African all-rounder Roy Pienaar appeared?

11   **FOUR**   Which batsman, now a famous radio commentator, scored the slowest fifty in Test history for England versus Australia at Brisbane in 1958–59?

12   **SIX**   Who captained Glamorgan to the County Championship title and was capped by Wales at rugby union?

13   **THREE**   Which prolific all-rounder took the wicket of Taslim Arif in 1979 to take his 100th Test wicket, only one year and 105 days after his debut?

14   **THREE**   Which famous all-rounder hit 138 for England in the 1st Test at Brisbane in 1986?

15   **SIX**   Which New Zealand all-rounder became the first player to score a hundred and take five wickets in a Test during the 2nd Test against India in 1964–65?

16   **SIX**   Which West Indian all-rounder scored 161 in seven hours at Edgbaston in 1957?

17   **THREE**   Who on 7 January 1987 dismissed Ratnayake of Sri Lanka to become only the second Test cricketer to score 3000 runs and take 300 wickets?

18   **FOUR**   Which Nottinghamshire player scored two hundreds and took 11–218 in the final County Championship game of 1988?

19   **TWO**   Who was the first player to hit four successive sixes in Test cricket?

20   **THREE**   Which Northamptonshire and England all-rounder played in the 1990 Nat West Trophy final despite a double fracture of a little finger?

21   **SIX**   Which former Essex all-rounder had a trial with baseball's Los Angeles Dodgers in 1987?

22   **FOUR**   Which all-rounder hit his first Test century for Pakistan against Australia in the 2nd Test at Adelaide in 1990?

23   **THREE**   Which all-rounder won the Man of the Match award in the 1986 and 1989 Nat West Trophy finals with different counties?

24   **FOUR**   For which county did South African Eddie Barlow play in the 1970s?

25   **FOUR**   Which Australian Test all-rounder signed for the Lancashire League club Nelson in 1987 and turned out for Somerset later that season?

SINGLES (5)   Name the five all-rounders who scored 500 runs and took 50 wickets in first-class matches in the 1992 season.

INNINGS SCORE:

KENT

1   **THREE**   Which future England bowler was awarded his county cap in 1964, the second youngest Kent player to receive the award?

2   **FOUR**   Which all-rounder took a hat-trick for the MCC against the Australians in 1972?

3   **SIX**   Which athletic fielder was Kent's county captain from 1978 to 1980?

4   **FOUR**   Where would you find the Nevill Cricket Ground?

5   **FOUR**   Which Kent batsman, who was better known as an umpire, scored 244 and 202* against Essex at Colchester in 1938?

6   **FOUR**   Which West Indian cricketer joined Kent in 1992?

7   **TWO**   Which Scottish-born batsman was named as Kent's skipper in 1971 and later captained England?

8   **THREE**   In which town would you be watching county cricket at Mote Park?

9   **THREE**   Which Kent wicket-keeper took seven catches on his Test debut at Trent Bridge in 1967?

10   **FOUR**   Which overseas batsman scored 89 versus Lancashire in the 1971 Gillette Cup final and was named Man of the Match?

11   **TWO**   Which cathedral city is Kent's cricketing headquarters?

12   **FOUR**   Which uncapped pace bowler toured Australia in 1979–80, aged just 20 years and 210 days, becoming the youngest England cricketer for 30 years?

13   **TWO**   Which England Test captain led Kent from 1957 to 1971?

14   **SIX**   Can you name the 6ft 7in Kent bowler who took 104 wickets in 1967?

15   **SIX**   Which left-handed batsman, often used as a deputy wicket-keeper for Alan Knott, scored 211 versus Derbyshire at Folkestone in 1963?

16   **THREE**   Kent tied for the 1977 County Championship with which other county?

17   **FOUR**   Which all-rounder scored 11 511 runs (av. 24.49) and took 512 wickets (av. 31.00) in the County Championship between 1965 and 1985 but never gained international honours?

18   **FOUR**   Which veteran bowler took 8–31 versus Scotland at Edinburgh in the 1987 Nat West Trophy?

19   **FOUR**   Which player has shared in the following stands: 366 with Simon Hinks (second wicket) and 300 with Mark Benson (first wicket)?

20   **SIX**   Which West Indian all-rounder played for Rhodesia in the 1975–76 Currie Cup competition whilst engaged to Kent CCC?

21   **THREE**   Who scored 47 868 runs for Kent between 1906 and 1938 and has taken the most catches by an outfield player?

22   **SIX**   Where would you be watching cricket if you were at Cheritan Road, Kent's only seaside ground?

23   **THREE**   Can you name the cricketer who was born in India, played for Pakistan and was Kent's captain in 1977?

24   **SIX**   Which current Kent cricketer scored 110 on his debut versus Sri Lanka at Canterbury in 1979?

25   **FOUR**   Which England opener scored 142 for Kent versus Somerset at Weston-Super-Mare in the 1970 Gillette Cup competition?

SINGLES (12) Between 1970 and 1993 twelve Kent players represented England. Name them.

INNINGS SCORE:

25

MODERN CRICKETING HEROES II

ALLAN BORDER

1 **FOUR** (*Two each*) For which two English sides did Allan Border appear?

2 **SIX** Which batsman started the 1986–87 Ashes series as Border's vice-captain?

3 **FOUR** Border came into the Australian Test side during the 1978–79 Ashes series. But who was his first captain?

4 **FOUR** (*Two each*) Which two Australian state sides has Border played for?

5 **SIX** Border's first Test wicket was that of an England captain. Name him.

6 **TWO** Who did Border succeed as Australian captain in 1984–85?

DAVID GOWER

7 **THREE** Who was David Gower's first captain at Leicestershire?

8 **FOUR** Where did Gower score 215 versus the Australians in 1985?

9 **THREE** Whom did Gower succeed as England captain for the Lord's Test versus Pakistan in 1982?

10 **SIX** What is David Gower's middle name?

11 **FOUR** Against which country did Gower make his Test debut in 1978?

12 **FOUR** Against which country did Gower achieve his first Test victory as captain?

DENNIS LILLEE

13 **THREE** For which English county did Lillee appear in the twilight of his career?

14 **FOUR** South Africa's tour of Australia in 1971 was cancelled for political reasons. Against whom did Lillee take 8–29 at Perth in a hastily-arranged series?

15   **THREE**   In the 1981–82 season, Lillee was banned from two one-day games after kicking which Pakistan batsman in a Test match?

16   **TWO**   In the 1979–80 Ashes series Lillee took his 100th English Test wicket. Who was the England skipper he dismissed?

17   **SIX**   In which calendar year did Lillee take 85 Test wickets at an average of 20.95?

18   **THREE**   At Melbourne in 1981–82, Lillee took 7–83 including a record 310th Test wicket (Larry Gomes). Which spinner previously held the aggregate record?

CLIVE LLOYD

19   **SIX**   Whom did Clive Lloyd succeed as Lancashire captain?

20   **FOUR**   When Lloyd hit 132 versus England in the 1st Test at the Oval in 1973, he resumed his innings the next day only to be dismissed first ball by which bowler?

21   **THREE**   Lloyd hit a splendid 126 in the 1972 Gillette Cup final against which county?

22   **TWO**   For which West Indian side did Lloyd play?

23   **THREE**   Which batsman did Lloyd replace as West Indies skipper?

24   **FOUR**   Who dismissed Lloyd in the 1986 Nat West Trophy final and went on to win the Man of the Match award?

25   **FOUR**   In which year did Lloyd make his Lancashire debut?

SINGLES (14) Between March and December 1984 Clive Lloyd led the West Indies to 11 successive Tests wins. Which 14 other players took part in this sequence?

INNINGS SCORE:

26

LEFT-HANDERS

1   **SIX**   Which left-arm seamer played for Kent in their 1971 Gillette Cup final defeat by Lancashire, and for Northamptonshire in their 1976 final win over the same county?

2   **FOUR**   Which left-handed batsman completed the double aged just 18 in 1949?

3   **FOUR**   During the 1990–91 Ashes tour Graham Gooch, the England captain, needed an operation on a septic finger. Which left-handed batsman flew out as his temporary replacement?

4   **TWO**   Name the slow left-arm bowler who took a wicket with his first ball in Test cricket against the West Indies at Trent Bridge in 1991.

5   **THREE**   Which left-handed batsman, captaining England for the only time in his career, scored 33 not out in two and a half hours at Sydney in 1971, despite suffering broken ribs after being hit in the body by a Dennis Lillee delivery?

6   **THREE**   Who, at Southport in 1982, scored two hundreds against Warwickshire, needing the aid of a runner in each innings?

7   **SIX**   Which New South Wales cricketer, who faced England for the first time in 1953, went on to score 750 runs and take 84 wickets in 25 Tests against them?

8   **SIX**   Which Surrey left-hander scored 149 not out in the 1991 Tilcon Trophy final, the highest ever score in the competition?

9   **TWO**   Which giant Australian left-arm pace bowler is the cousin of New Zealander John Reid?

10   **FOUR**   Which batsman and former captain of Australia hit 1418 runs (av. 67.52) in the 1982–83 season to beat Bill Ponsford's 55 year-old Sheffield Shield run aggregate record?

11   **THREE**   Which Australian opening batsman completed 1000 runs in Ashes Tests, in only his 17th Test innings, during the 3rd Test at Sydney in 1990–91?

12   **TWO**   Which famous England left-hander was born in Tunbridge Wells on April Fool's Day 1957?

13   **FOUR**   Name the Yorkshire batsman who hit 260 not out for England Young Cricketers versus the West Indies in 1977, a batting record for England in Youth Test matches.

14   **SIX**   Which current Surrey left-hander played football for England Schools against Scotland?

15   **SIX**   Name the Australian left-arm swing bowler who took 6–34 against England in the Perth Test of 1979–80.

16   **THREE**   Which opening batsman, who is now a radio commentator, hit 214 not out versus India at Edgbaston in 1974 in only his second Test?

17   **THREE**   Which slow bowler took five wickets in the 3rd Test at Sydney in 1990–91, in only his second England appearance?

18   **FOUR**   Can you name the batsman who hit his fifth hundred in Roses matches for Lancashire at Headingley in 1992?

19   **THREE**   Who captained Somerset to five one-day titles during his captaincy from 1978 to 1983?

20   **FOUR**   Which South Australian left-handed batsman, aged just 21, hit five hundreds in six innings in the 1976–77 season?

21   **THREE**   Name the former England opener who hit ten consecutive scoring strokes for six whilst playing for Lancashire against Leicestershire at Old Trafford in 1983.

22   **SIX**   Which left-arm pace bowler, who played Test cricket for England in the 1960s, is now a travel agent specialising in tours of the Caribbean?

23   **FOUR**   Which Australian left-hander, who was the youngest member of their touring party, scored 112 in his first Test appearance against England at Headingley in 1948?

24   **THREE**   Which England batsman was named International Cricketer of the Year in 1987?

25   **FOUR**   Which recently retired left-arm bowler had the initials J K?

SINGLES (14) Fourteen batsman batted left-handed in Tests for England in the 1980s. Name them.

INNINGS SCORE:

27

LANCASHIRE

1 **FOUR** Which diminutive batsman scored 625 runs in the 1970 John Player League?

2 **SIX** Who dismissed Don Bradman twice in the 1948 Lancashire versus Australia match?

3 **SIX** When Wasim Akram left the field in the County Championship match against Warwickshire at Old Trafford in May 1989, which former Lancashire and England player replaced him, ten years after leaving the county?

4 **FOUR** Which former England batsman was Lancashire county captain from 1978 to 1980?

5 **THREE** Which veteran Lancashire spinner was dropped and fined for comments made after the Roses game in June 1987?

6 **SIX** Who took a hat-trick for Lancashire in the 1968 Roses match at Leeds?

7 **TWO** For which other county has Gehan Mendis played?

8 **SIX** Which Lancashire left-handed batsman was named Young Player of the Year in 1975?

9 **THREE** Can you name Lance Gibbs' cousin who has played for the county?

10 **FOUR** Who scored 34 off a Malcolm Nash over at Swansea in 1977?

11 **THREE** Who took over the county captaincy when Jack Bond retired in 1972?

12 **FOUR** Which England pace bowler took 1816 wickets for the county between 1950 and 1968?

13 **SIX** Which Lancastrian all-rounder scored a hundred off just 61 balls in the 1991 Roses match to record the fastest first-class century of the season?

14 **TWO** Who scored 100 in 35 minutes against Leicestershire at Manchester in 1983 to equal the world record for the fastest first-class century?

15 **FOUR** Which West Indian bowler took 6–10 against Scotland at Manchester in the 1982 Benson & Hedges Cup?

16 **FOUR** Which Lancashire cricketer was named as a Wisden Cricketer of the Year in 1987 despite only scoring 422 runs and taking just two wickets?

17 **SIX** Who, at Trent Bridge in 1990, scored 106 against Nottinghamshire on his County Championship debut?

18 **FOUR** Who, at Taunton back in 1895, scored 424 for Lancashire against Somerset?

19 **TWO** Who hit 366 versus Surrey at the Oval in 1990, recording the second highest score by a Lancashire player?

20 **THREE** Who took 112 wickets for the county in 1975?

21 **FOUR** When Lancashire beat Worcestershire in the 1990 Benson & Hedges Cup final, who was named Man of the Match?

22 **SIX** Can you name the Dane who made his county debut in 1985?

23 **THREE** Which West Indian Test cricketer made his Lancashire debut in 1981 whilst appearing for Rishton in the Lancashire League?

24 **SIX** Who is the only batsman to score 2000 runs in a season without scoring a first-class century?

25 **FOUR** Which former England opener wrote the book entitled *Fox on the Run*, named by Channel 4 as a sports book of the year?

SINGLES (11) Name the Lancashire side that beat Sussex to win the 1970 Gillette Cup final.

INNINGS SCORE:

ENGLAND V PAKISTAN

1 **FOUR** Which batsman deputised for wicket-keeper Alec Stewart on the first day of the 5th Test at the Oval in 1992?

2 **FOUR** Which Pakistan batsman scored 274 at Edgbaston in 1971 and 240 at the Oval in 1974?

3 **THREE** (*One run each*) Name the three Mohammed brothers who have played cricket for Pakistan against England.

4 **THREE** Name the Yorkshireman who was called up to keep wicket for England in the fourth Texaco Trophy game at Lord's in 1992.

5 **TWO** Name the 1992 Pakistan team manager who put on 190 for the ninth wicket with Asif Iqbal at the Oval in 1967.

6 **FOUR** Who, at Trent Bridge in 1992, captained Pakistan for the third one-day international when Javed Miandad pulled out ill?

7 **SIX** Who captained England in Pakistan for the 1961–62 series?

8 **SIX** Which member of the 1992 Pakistan touring side scored 19 hundreds for East Kilbride in 1990 and 1991?

9 **FOUR** Which young all-rounder joined the 1974 Pakistan tourists after finishing his summer term at Oxford University?

10 **SIX** Which Pakistan batsman missed the first few matches of their 1987 England tour whilst waiting for the birth of his child?

11 **TWO** Aqib Javed was fined half his match fee for showing dissent to which umpire in the 3rd Test in 1992?

12 **THREE** Which Pakistan batsman compiled 205 on the first day of the 3rd Test in 1992, to hit only the fourth double century in Tests at Old Trafford?

13 **THREE** England amassed 363–7 versus Pakistan in the fourth Texaco Trophy game in 1992, the highest ever one-day international score. Which team previously held the record?

14 **FOUR** Where did Pakistan score 708 versus England in 1987?

15 **TWO** Which wicket-keeper captained Pakistan on their 1978 tour of England?

16   **SIX**   Ted Munton and Ian Salisbury made their England Test debuts in 1992. Coincidentally their first Test dismissals involved the same batsman. Who?

17   **SIX**   Which legendary England batsman hit 278 against Pakistan at Trent Bridge in 1954?

18   **THREE**   Which Kent and England player was robbed of his first Test century by rioting at Dacca during the 1968–69 series?

19   **SIX**   Which 17 year-old took 3–69 on his Test debut for Pakistan at Edgbaston in 1992?

20   **TWO**   Which batsman scored 69 not out in 1992 to become the first Englishman to carry his bat in a Lord's Test?

21   **FOUR**   Name the seldom-used bowler who took 6–32 in Pakistan's victory at Lord's in 1982.

22   **SIX**   Which England spinner had match figures of 11–83 in the 1st Test at Karachi in 1983–84?

23   **THREE**   At Headingley in 1992 England fielded seven recognised batsmen. Who came in at number seven?

24   **TWO**   Who, aged 30, took 8–122 in the 1992 Headingley Test to record the best debut match figures by an English bowler since John Lever's 10–70 at Delhi in 1976?

25   **FOUR**   In the 1992 series, who surprisingly topped the England bowling averages with five wickets at an average of 18.80?

SINGLES (10) England skipper Mike Gatting was involved in an infamous row with Shakoor Rana at Faisalabad in December 1987. Name the other ten members of the England side.

INNINGS SCORE:

29

CAPTAINS

1   **TWO**   Who resigned as captain of Essex in 1987, claiming the extra responsibility had affected his batting?

2   **FOUR**   Who skippered England on the successful tour of the West Indies in 1967–68?

3   **THREE**   Who was the first professional captain of England?

4   **FOUR**   Which former Australian Test captain scored 11 sixes in one innings for a TN Pearce XI versus Scarborough in 1953?

5   **SIX**   Name the winning captain in the 1988 Nat West Trophy final who was run out without facing a ball.

6   **THREE**   Who in 1988 was dismissed as captain at Gloucestershire just hours after taking career-best match figures of 14–165?

7   **FOUR**   Who led Surrey to the 1971 County Championship title?

8   **THREE**   During the 1988 series versus the West Indies, England appointed four different captains: John Emburey, Mike Gatting, Graham Gooch and who else?

9   **TWO**   In 1981, who led Nottinghamshire to their first County Championship title in 52 years?

10   **FOUR**   Which Australian Test skipper had the middle name of Baddeley?

11   **SIX**   Who led Glamorgan to their second County Championship title in 1969?

12   **FOUR**   The captains in the 5th England–West Indies Test in 1980 played for the same English county. Name the county.

13   **THREE**   Who led Sussex to victory in the first two Gillette Cup finals?

14   **SIX**   Who in 1978–79, aged just 25 and in only his 11th Test, skippered Australia against Pakistan after Graham Yallop had withdrawn injured?

15   **SIX**   Whose autobiography entitled *Captain's Story*, published in 1966, was withdrawn owing to comments made about Ian Meckiff, a fast bowler who had been no-balled in Test matches for throwing?

16 **FOUR** Who skippered England in the 1979 World Cup final?

17 **THREE** Which captain lost the Ashes Test at Brisbane in 1990, his third defeat in three Tests as England skipper?

18 **FOUR** Who replaced Clive Lloyd as captain of the West Indies when Lloyd joined Kerry Packer's World Series in 1978?

19 **FOUR** Who retired from Test cricket in 1964 after captaining Australia in 28 of his 63 Test matches, never losing a Test rubber as skipper?

20 **FOUR** Who captained South Africa in the unofficial Tests against Mike Gatting's rebel XI in 1990?

21 **FOUR** Surrey wrapped up the 1957 County Championship title by 16 August. Who was their successful captain?

22 **THREE** Who led the England rebel tourists to South Africa in 1982?

23 **THREE** Who was the Australian skipper in the 1981 Headingley Test who enforced the follow-on only to see England fight back to win?

24 **TWO** Name the Indian captain who accused English bowlers of applying vaseline to the ball in Madras in 1976–77.

25 **TWO** Who was recalled to the Test arena to captain England on the tour of India in 1981–82?

SINGLES (20) As at 1 January 1993, which 20 players have captained England in Ashes Tests since the Second World War?

INNINGS SCORE:

30

ENGLAND V WEST INDIES

1   **THREE**   Which pace bowler, nicknamed 'Whispering Death', took 28 wickets in the 1976 series at an average of just 12.71?

2   **SIX**   Which Lancastrian batsman hit 106* in the 1st Test of the 1973 series but failed to score a half-century in any of his remaining 15 Test innings, all against the West Indies?

3   **FOUR**   Which English batsman took Phil Simmons' wicket with only his third ball in Test cricket at Lord's in 1991?

4   **TWO**   Name the England batsman who scored centuries in three successive Tests in 1984.

5   **THREE**   Which English opener scored 2205 runs against the West Indies in 29 matches, disproving critics who claimed he avoided fast bowling?

6   **SIX**   Which pace bowler made his West Indies debut in the 2nd Test at Lord's in 1991?

7   **THREE**   Which diminutive batsman hit 98 for the West Indies in the 3rd Test at Port of Spain in 1990, after going out to bat with the score at 29–5?

8   **SIX**   Which all-rounder deputised as skipper when Graham Gooch went off the field against the West Indies at the Oval in 1988?

9   **THREE**   Which batsman became only the sixth Englishman to carry his bat in Tests when he hit 154 not out at Headingley in 1991?

10   **FOUR**   Which pace bowler took 24 off an Ian Botham over at Port of Spain, Trinidad in 1981?

11   **FOUR**   Which Englishman hit 262 not out in the drawn Test at Kingston in 1973–74?

12   **FOUR**   Which left-handed batsman, who was the first English-registered player to score 1000 first-class runs that season, made his England debut versus the West Indies at Edgbaston in 1991?

13   **SIX**   Which Sussex left-hander, a renowned player of fast bowling, was named as Graham Gooch's replacement when the England captain had his hand broken in the 1990 Trinidad Test.

14 **SIX** Which Surrey pace bowler took a hat-trick at Leeds in 1957, the first for England in a home Test since 1899?

15 **THREE** Name the West Indian batsman, most famous for a spectacular start to his Test career, who hit 302 at Bridgetown in the 1973–74 series.

16 **FOUR** Which young England batsman had his arm broken by a Winston Davis delivery at Old Trafford in 1984, but returned with his arm strapped up to try to save the follow-on?

17 **THREE** Who, at the Oval in 1991, took 6–25 to force the West Indies to follow-on for the first time in England since 1969?

18 **FOUR** Which gutsy England batsman scored 100 not out at the Oval in 1980, taking part in an undefeated tenth-wicket partnership of 117 with Bob Willis that saved the game?

19 **FOUR** (*Two runs each*) Geoff Boycott was dismissed seven times in Tests by two West Indian bowlers. Name them.

20 **SIX** Which famous batsman played against England at Kingston in 1953–54 aged 44 years and 236 days, to become the oldest ever West Indian Test cricketer?

21 **TWO** Which legendary batsman made his last ever Test appearance at the Oval in 1991?

22 **THREE** Which pace bowler broke his thumb fielding at Leeds in 1984, then not only came into bat one-handed to ensure Larry Gomes got his hundred but also took his finest Test figures of 7–53?

23 **FOUR** Which Warwickshire batsman hit 10* on his home ground in 1984 before being hit on the side of the head by a Malcolm Marshall delivery and missing the rest of the season?

24 **SIX** Who, at the Oval in 1966, shared a tenth-wicket partnership of 128 with John Snow?

25 **FOUR** Which West Indies pace bowler joined the 1984 tour of England as a late replacement and scored 77 as a night-watchman in the Old Trafford Test?

SINGLES (11) When England beat the West Indies at Sabina Park in 1990 it was their first win against this opposition for 16 years. Name the victorious side.

INNINGS SCORE:

PICTURE QUIZ 3

1   **FOUR**   Name this ▲
distinctive county ground.

2   **FOUR**   Where is this idyllic
Test match ground? ▶

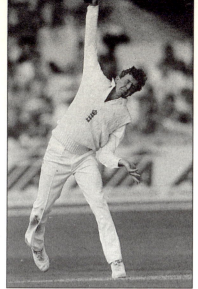

3

FOUR Who is this England Test cricketer displaying an unusual bowling action? ◀

4a **TWO** Name the England batsman who has just been given out. ▶

4b **TWO** Who is the successful Indian bowler?

4c **FOUR** What has the batsman just done?

5 **SINGLES** (16) Identify the England players on this team photograph of the 1981/82 tour of India and Sri Lanka.

INNINGS SCORE:

31 LEICESTERSHIRE

1   **TWO**   Who, on 15 September 1975, played cricket for Leicestershire against Derbyshire at Chesterfield (11.30am to 6.30pm) and soccer for Doncaster Rovers versus Brentford at Doncaster (7.30pm to 9.10pm)?

2   **FOUR**   Which former England bowler partnered Ray Illingworth in a tenth wicket stand of 228 versus Northamptonshire at Leicester in 1977?

3   **SIX**   Which Leicestershire batsman was 12th man for England against the Rest of the World at Lord's in 1970, just one month after making his first-class debut?

4   **SIX**   Which wicket-keeper scored 103 for Leicestershire against Middlesex in a 1972 John Player League game at Lord's but was dismissed for obstructing the field?

5   **FOUR**   Which current first-class umpire scored 152 at Old Trafford in a 1975 John Player League game?

6   **FOUR**   Which overseas cricketer scored seven hundreds for the county in the 1982 season?

7   **SIX**   Leicestershire were bowled out for 56 in a 1982 Benson & Hedges zonal game by a non-county side. Name the opposition.

8   **THREE**   Which Leicestershire batsman was named Young Player of the Year in 1978?

9   **FOUR**   Which famous England spin bowler joined the county as player-coach in 1965?

10   **THREE**   Which Australian resigned as Leicestershire's cricket manager at the end of 1991?

11   **FOUR**   Which Leicestershire all-rounder played for Leicester City at half-back in the 1969 FA Cup final?

12   **FOUR**   Which England spin bowler took 111 wickets for the county in 1967?

13   **TWO**   Which famous Leicestershire and England captain was awarded the CBE in the 1973 New Year's Honours List?

14   **FOUR**   Which Australian bowler took hat-tricks in two limited overs games in 1972?

15   **SIX**   Which Leicestershire fast bowler took 9–37 at Derby in 1991, recording the best County Championship figures for 16 years?

16   **FOUR**   Which overseas cricketer scored 158 not out for Leicestershire against Warwickshire at Coventry in the 1972 Benson & Hedges Cup?

17   **THREE**   Which Ceylon-born cricketer scored 51 in just eight minutes against Nottinghamshire at Trent Bridge in 1965?

18   **TWO**   Which England all-rounder left the county at the end of the 1991 season?

19   **FOUR**   Which Leicestershire player took a hat-trick in the 1974 Benson & Hedges Cup final versus Surrey?

20   **FOUR**   Leicestershire scored just six hundreds in the 1992 County Championship. Who was the only batsman to reach three figures twice?

21   **FOUR**   Which West Indian bowler took a hat-trick against the touring Australians in 1989?

22   **FOUR**   Who in 1986 was named Young Player of the Year and was selected to tour Australia that winter?

23   **SIX**   Which current umpire kept wicket for the county between 1953 and 1971?

24   **THREE**   Peter Willey joined Leicestershire in 1984, but for which county had he previously appeared?

25   **THREE**   Who made his Leicestershire debut in 1971, aged just 16, and has captained the side since 1990?

SINGLES (11) Leicestershire beat Yorkshire by five wickets to win the first Benson & Hedges Cup final in 1972. Name their side.

INNINGS SCORE:

WICKET-KEEPERS

1   **FOUR**   Which Indian wicket-keeper took a Test record five stumpings in one innings versus the West Indies in 1987?

2   **SIX**   Which England wicket-keeper took seven catches in the Ashes Test at Old Trafford in 1961?

3   **THREE**   Which Lancashire wicket-keeper, who was only third choice at the start of the 1987 season, came into bat as a night-watchman against Nottinghamshire in July 1987 and scored 130?

4   **THREE**   Name the wicket-keeper who scored 173 for New Zealand against India in the 3rd Test at Auckland in 1990, registering the highest score by a number nine batsman in Test cricket history.

5   **FOUR**   (*One run each*) Which four players kept wicket for England in the Lord's Test against New Zealand in 1986?

6   **SIX**   Which famous wicket-keeper stumped a record 415 batsmen between 1926 and 1950?

7   **THREE**   Name the Essex wicket-keeper who scored two centuries in September 1991 to help his county to the Championship title.

8   **TWO**   Who kept wicket for England in the famous Ashes Test at Headingley in 1981?

9   **SIX**   What unique achievement did WH Brain attain at Cheltenham in 1893?

10   **FOUR**   Who took eight catches for Pakistan in the 1971 Test match at Leeds?

11   **TWO**   Who, at Chesterfield in 1963, took ten catches for Derbyshire against Hampshire?

12   **FOUR**   Who scored 606 runs for South Africa against Australia in the 1966–67 home Test series?

13   **FOUR**   Which Kent wicket-keeper played for England 'A' against Sri Lanka at Old Trafford in 1991?

14   **FOUR**   Against which country did Jack Russell make his Test debut?

15   **TWO**   Who was just 25 years 120 days old when he made his 100th Test match dismissal for England on 7 August 1971?

16   **THREE**   Which wicket-keeper, more renowned for his batting power, made 80 dismissals for Warwickshire in the 1985 season?

17   **SIX**   Who took 96 catches for Yorkshire in 1960?

18   **TWO**   Which England wicket-keeper took a hat-trick of catches for Gloucestershire against Surrey at the Oval in September 1986?

19   **SIX**   Which former England and Leicestershire wicket-keeper led Old Malvernians to the 1986 Cricketer Cup?

20   **THREE**   Who made 24 dismissals for the West Indies in their 1963 Test series in England?

21   **SIX**   Who made 1294 dismissals for Essex between 1949 and 1973?

22   **FOUR**   Which wicket-keeper toured Australia in 1982–83 as understudy to Bob Taylor and has made 18 one-day international appearances?

23   **SIX**   Who kept wicket for Australia in the 1986 tied Test at Madras?

24   **SIX**   Which former Derby County goalkeeper kept wicket for Goatacre in the 1990 village cricket final?

25   **FOUR**   When Jim Laker took 19 Test wickets versus Australia at Old Trafford in 1956, who was the famous England wicket-keeper who made just one dismissal?

SINGLES (7)   Name the seven men selected to keep wicket for England in Test matches in the 1980s.

INNINGS SCORE:

33

PAKISTAN

1   **FOUR**   Which all-rounder, who played county cricket for Northamptonshire, took 7–59 for Pakistan against Middlesex at Lord's in 1974?

2   **SIX**   Who scored 2991 runs for his country between 1958 and 1971 in 41 Tests?

3   **FOUR**   Who took 77 wickets on the 1954 tour of England?

4   **SIX**   When Hanif Mohammed scored 499 for Karachi against Bahawalpur at Karachi, how was he out?

5   **THREE**   Who, at Lahore in December 1977, scored a Test match hundred in 557 minutes for Pakistan against England?

6   **FOUR**   Which Pakistan all-rounder, who has recently acted as their tour manager, played in all five matches for the Rest of the World versus England in 1970?

7   **THREE**   Which pace bowler took 9–86 for Pakistan versus Australia in Melbourne in 1978–79?

8   **SIX**   Which Pakistan Test cricketer was dismissed for obstructing the field whilst playing for Warwickshire against Hampshire at Coventry in 1963?

9   **TWO**   Who, aged just 29, became Pakistan's leading Test run-scorer during their 1986 tour of Sri Lanka?

10   **SIX**   Which legendary batsman was 17 years 300 days old when he kept wicket for Pakistan in their first Test match versus India in 1952, the youngest player ever to keep wicket in a Test match?

11   **SIX**   Can you name the Pakistan all-rounder who was Dennis Lillee's 300th Test match victim?

12   **TWO**   Which country beat Pakistan in the 1979 and 1983 World Cup semi-finals?

13   **THREE**   Who, aged just 18, made his Pakistan Test debut at Birmingham in 1971?

14   **SIX**   When Pakistan toured New Zealand in 1989, which side bowled them out for 48 in a tour game?

15   **SIX**   Which Pakistan bowler delivered five bouncers in one over to Nottinghamshire's Jon Birch in a tour game in 1987 and received two warnings from umpire Barry Dudleston?

16   **SIX**   Which county beat the touring Pakistanis in May 1987 by an innings and 57 runs?

17   **FOUR**   Who, at Karachi in 1976–77, scored a hundred before lunch on the first day of the Pakistan versus New Zealand Test?

18   **FOUR**   Who captained his country in 17 Tests from 1969 to 1975?

19   **THREE**   Which batsman notched up his 4000th one-day international run in the fourth Texaco Trophy game at Lord's in 1992?

20   **SIX**   Name the Pakistan wicket-keeper/opener who scored 210 not out in the 2nd Test against Australia at Faisalabad in 1978–79.

21   **SIX**   In which city is the National Stadium?

22   **THREE**   When both Javed Miandad and Salim Malik were ruled out of the fifth one-day international at Old Trafford in 1992, who captained the side?

23   **THREE**   Who, at Karachi in 1959–60, became the only Pakistan cricketer to take a wicket with his first ball in Test cricket?

24   **FOUR**   Who hit 260 out of Pakistan's 708 at the Oval in 1987?

25   **THREE**   Which Pakistan wicket-keeper dismissed his 100th Test victim at Kingston, Jamaica in 1977?

SINGLES (11) In December 1970, a Pakistan XI played a Rest of the World side at Karachi in aid of the Flood Disaster fund. Name their team.

INNINGS SCORE:

34

BATTING II

1 **THREE** (*One run each*) Against the West Indies at Manchester in 1963, the first three England batsmen were all Surrey players. Name them.

2 **THREE** Which New Zealand batsman hit 171 versus East Africa in the 1975 World Cup?

3 **TWO** Who in November 1989, aged just 16 years 214 days, became the youngest Test cricketer to score a fifty?

4 **FOUR** Which Englishman took 350 minutes to score the second slowest fifty in first-class cricket versus Pakistan at Lord's in 1982?

5 **FOUR** Which Australian batsman and future skipper became the first Test player to wear a helmet in Test cricket during the 1977–78 Bridgetown Test?

6 **THREE** Who in August 1991 hit 174 versus Sri Lanka, notching up his sixth century at Lord's?

7 **FOUR** Which cricketer, who represented England in one-day cricket, hit 122 not out versus Oxford University in his only first-class game of the 1991 season?

8 **THREE** Which Pakistan Test cricketer hit a double hundred at Neath against the 1985 Australians to become the first Glamorgan player to reach that score on four occasions?

9 **FOUR** David Gower is widely remembered for his Tiger Moth stunt at Queensland during the 1990–91 Ashes Tour. But which batsman accompanied him on his flight?

10 **TWO** Who passed Sir Garfield Sobers' Test run aggregate record for the West Indies (8032) in the 1991 Kingston Test versus Australia?

11 **THREE** Which English batsman scored the slowest ever Ashes hundred during the 3rd Test at Sydney in 1990–91?

12 **FOUR** Which promising Essex batsman scored 243 versus Leicestershire at Chelmsford in 1990, recording their eighth highest County Championship innings score?

13 **TWO** Which Northamptonshire and England batsman hit 30 (6.4.4.6.6.4) off an Alvin Kallicharran over at Edgbaston in 1982?

14   **THREE**   Which England batsman hit 200 not out versus India at Edgbaston in 1979 to complete 1000 Test runs in only his 13th Test?

15   **THREE**   Who in 1982 hit 311 not out for Worcestershire against Warwickshire to become only the second non-Englishman to hit 100 first-class hundreds?

16   **TWO**   Which Nottinghamshire opener hit 934 runs (av. 62.27) in his first 11 Tests after making his England debut on the 1984–85 tour of India?

17   **SIX**   Which young Australian batsman hit 6 sixes off an over whilst playing club cricket for Dulwich in 1976?

18   **SIX**   Which New Zealand batsman, who was born in Lancashire, hit 116 versus England at Trent Bridge in 1973 as his side narrowly missed reaching the total of 479 needed to win?

19   **FOUR**   Which Englishman scored a hundred at Melbourne on 8 June 1929 aged 46 years 82 days, and still remains the oldest Test cricketer to hit a century?

20   **THREE**   Which current England Test selector hit 179 against India at Delhi in 1976, reaching his hundred with a six, for the highest score by an Englishman in India until the record was broken in 1984–85?

21   **FOUR**   (*Two runs each*) Which two Worcestershire batsmen hit centuries before lunch against Warwickshire at Worcester in 1979, the first such occurrence in 24 years?

22   **THREE**   Who in 1976–77, in only his third Test match, hit 206 against New Zealand to become, at 19 years 4 months, the youngest ever to hit a Test double century?

23   **FOUR**   Which county scored 23 centuries during the 1991 County Championship season but still finished bottom of the table?

24   **THREE**   Which Hampshire opener, who at the start of the season was unsure of a first-team place, became the first batsman to reach 1000 first-class runs in 1992?

25   **TWO**   Who took over the Worcestershire captaincy on 30 July 1991 and had scored 2000 first-class runs within 11 months?

SINGLES (6) Which six non-Englishmen have hit triple centuries in Test matches?

INNINGS SCORE:

35

MIDDLESEX

1   **FOUR**   When Paul Downton retired from first-class cricket in 1991, which former Kent stumper initially replaced him as Middlesex wicket-keeper?

2   **FOUR**   Name the Trinidadian left-hander who made his Middlesex debut in 1973.

3   **SIX**   Who scored 13 centuries for Middlesex in 1947?

4   **THREE**   Which Middlesex and England captain scored 4310 runs for Cambridge University between 1961 and 1964?

5   **THREE**   Spinner Alex Barnett left Middlesex at the end of 1991 to join which county?

6   **THREE**   Which former England spinner shared a sixth-wicket partnership of 227 with Clive Radley against the South Africans at Lord's in 1967?

7   **TWO**   Which Middlesex batsman was elected Young Player of the Year in 1981?

8   **FOUR**   Mike Selvey made his Middlesex debut in 1972. For which county had he previously appeared?

9   **THREE**   Which young batsman was named Man of the Match when Middlesex beat Worcestershire in the 1988 Nat West Trophy final?

10   **FOUR**   Which pace bowler was elected Young Cricketer of the Year in 1982 and was chosen to tour Australia that winter?

11   **FOUR**   Which left-handed batsman scored 158 versus Lancashire in a Nat West Trophy game at Lord's in 1984?

12   **THREE**   Who in 1957 completed the wicket-keeping double (104 dismissals and 1025 runs) to become only the second keeper to achieve this milestone?

13   **FOUR**   Name the England batsman who scored three successive centuries against Pakistan in 1962.

14   **THREE**   Which overseas bowler took 51 wickets in all forms of limited-overs cricket in 1981 to equal RJ Clapp's (Somerset) record of 1974?

15 **FOUR** Which fast bowler made his debut for the county in 1989 after seven years with Worcestershire and was so impressive he gained selection for England's 1990 West Indies tour?

16 **TWO** Name the spin bowler who took 103 wickets for Middlesex in 1983 and was named as a Wisden Cricketer of the Year.

17 **FOUR** Mike Gatting has a footballing brother called Steve. For which team did Steve play in an FA Cup final?

18 **TWO** Which overseas batsman hit 255 not out versus Sussex at Lord's in 1990, registering the eighth highest score for Middlesex?

19 **FOUR** Which current Durham bowler took wickets with his last two balls of the 1990 first-class season and had to wait seven months for a hat-trick attempt?

20 **SIX** In which country was Phil Edmonds born?

21 **FOUR** Which bowler, who is the son and grandson of West Indian Test cricketers, picked up the wicket of Yorkshire's Ashley Metcalfe in the first game of the 1991 season with his first ball in County Championship cricket?

22 **FOUR** From which county did Andy Needham join Middlesex in 1987?

23 **FOUR** Who took 2361 wickets for Middlesex from 1949 to 1982?

24 **SIX** Which Middlesex pace bowler, with a unique run-up, was awarded his county cap in 1963 and ended the season by being selected to tour India?

25 **THREE** With whom were Middlesex joint County Champions in 1949?

SINGLES (15) Between 1 January 1970 and 31 December 1989 fifteen Middlesex players played for England. Name them.

INNINGS SCORE:

36

VENUES

1   **SIX**   At which ground did the West Indies play their first match of the 1991 England tour?

2   **FOUR**   Two county grounds have entrances named after WG Grace; one is at Lord's but where else are there 'Grace Gates'?

3   **FOUR**   Which county plays at Moreton-in-Marsh?

4   **TWO**   On which ground did Ian Botham make his Test debut?

5   **THREE**   Where was the first one-day international held in England?

6   **SIX**   Which minor county played Middlesex at St George's, Telford in a Nat West Trophy game in 1992?

7   **FOUR**   Which county played at Dean Park for the last time in 1992 after a 95-year association?

8   **TWO**   Where did Pakistan beat England to win the 1992 World Cup final?

9   **THREE**   When Paris staged the 1900 Olympic Games, who beat the host nation in the only ever Olympic cricket final?

10   **THREE**   In which city do Hampshire play county cricket at the United Services Officers' ground?

11   **FOUR**   Where was the 1987 World Cup final held?

12   **THREE**   Where was an Ashes Test match abandoned in 1970–71 without a ball being bowled?

13   **THREE**   Where is the WACA ground?

14   **SIX**   Middlesex moved their headquarters to Lord's in 1876, but where had they previously been?

15   **THREE**   In 1890 and 1938 Ashes Tests were abandoned without a ball being bowled. Where were both these matches due to be staged?

16   **FOUR**   On which English ground did Australia score 721 in one day in 1948?

17   **SIX**   At which North American venue did the West Indies beat England by seven wickets in a one-day game in September 1990?

18   **TWO**   Where was the 1st Test between England and the West Indies staged in 1957, 28 years after a Test was last staged there?

19   **TWO**   Which English ground has lost most complete days of Test cricket to rain?

20   **SIX**   Essex were docked 25 points in the 1989 County Championship for preparing an unsuitable pitch. At which venue?

21   **FOUR**   South Africa returned to the Test match scene in the West Indies in 1992 after a 22-year exile. Where was this Test match held?

22   **SIX**   Which county played at Hesketh Park until 1991?

23   **THREE**   On which ground did Graeme Hick score 405 not out in 1988?

24   **THREE**   Which county plays cricket at Uxbridge?

25   **FOUR**   On which Test match ground would you find the Warwick Road end?

SINGLES (6) In 1992, during their debut first-class season, Durham staged cricket at which six venues?

INNINGS SCORE:

37

MILESTONES

1   **FOUR**   Whose duck in the 2nd Test at Melbourne in 1990 was his first in a record 119 successive Test innings?

2   **SIX**   When Sir Gary Sobers scored his Test record innings of 365, wicket-keeper Imtiaz Ahmed didn't remove his gloves. Who was the only other Pakistan cricketer not to bowl?

3   **FOUR**   Who in 1965 at Trent Bridge, aged just 21, became the youngest batsman to complete 1000 Test runs?

4   **FOUR**   Who in 1987 became only the second Northamptonshire-born cricketer to play for England?

5   **FOUR**   Who was the last cricketer to score 2000 runs and take 100 wickets in an English first-class season?

6   **SIX**   Where did both Viv Richards and Don Bradman score their 100th first-class centuries?

7   **THREE**   Which Hampshire bowler took four wickets in five balls, including a hat-trick, against Lancashire in May 1992?

8   **TWO**   Who completed the double in 1988 and was named Britannic Assurance Cricketer of the Year?

9   **SIX**   Which South African became the first bowler to take all ten wickets in an innings in the Lancashire League for 24 years when he achieved the feat in 1988?

10   **TWO**   Where did Sir Gary Sobers score his Test innings of 365?

11   **THREE**   Which Australian was Fred Trueman's 300th wicket in Test cricket?

12   **SIX**   Who made his Pakistan debut versus New Zealand in 1989, aged only 16 years 190 days?

13   **TWO**   In 1990 England beat the West Indies in a Test match for the time in 16 years. Who hit the winning run?

14   **FOUR**   Which New Zealander took 94 minutes to get off the mark versus Australia at Wellington in 1990?

15   **THREE**   Which Indian batsman was Richard Hadlee's 400th Test match victim?

16   **SIX**   Who scored an amazing 77 runs off a Rob Vance over for Canterbury versus Wellington in 1990?

17   **THREE**   Who did Cambridge University beat in July 1990 for their first win against a county in eight years?

18   **FOUR**   Which Nottinghamshire and England batsman was the first player to get two pairs on different pitches in the same first-class game?

19   **TWO**   Which Hampshire bowler took his 1500th first-class wicket (David Smith) against Sussex in July 1992?

20   **TWO**   Which wicket-keeper passed Alan Knott's Test record of 263 dismissals during the 1981 Headingley Test?

21   **SIX**   During the 1st England-Pakistan Test in 1987, umpire Dickie Bird became the first official to retire hurt. Which former England Test player replaced him?

22   **FOUR**   Chris Broad has scored Test centuries at four of the six Australian Test grounds. Apart from the Bellerive Oval, which is the only other venue where he hasn't reached three figures?

23   **THREE**   Which English bowler conceded 200 runs in a Test innings versus Pakistan in the final Test of 1987, only the second Test bowler to be so expensive?

24   **THREE**   Who recorded the best Test figures for a debutant for India versus West Indies at Chepauk in 1987?

25   **THREE**   Wally Hammond's England Test run-aggregate record stood at 7249 runs until which player surpassed it on 29 November 1970?

SINGLES (5) Name the five batsmen who have scored more than 150 first-class centuries.

INNINGS SCORE:

38

NORTHAMPTONSHIRE

1 **FOUR** Which future England batsman took a hat-trick against the Combined Universities in the 1980 Benson & Hedges Cup?

2 **SIX** Who scored 28 980 runs for the county between 1934 and 1959?

3 **THREE** Who scored 102 for the Indians against Northamptonshire in 1979 and joined the county two years later?

4 **FOUR** Which Pakistani took 101 wickets for the county in the 1975 season?

5 **FOUR** Which Pakistani cricketer won the 1965 single-wicket tournament at Lord's?

6 **FOUR** Which future England batsman took 8–29 versus Lancashire at Northampton in 1966, bowling left-arm spin?

7 **FOUR** Who in 1991 became the fourth Northamptonshire player to reach 20 000 runs for the county?

8 **THREE** Nick Cook joined the county in 1986. For which side had he previously appeared?

9 **FOUR** Which Northamptonshire all-rounder scored 134 for Eastern Province against Western Province at Port Elizabeth in 1986–87?

10 **THREE** Which fast bowler took 7–75 against his former county, Glamorgan, at Northampton in 1990?

11 **FOUR** Which Northamptonshire batsman was elected Young Cricketer of the Year in 1984?

12 **FOUR** Which Northern county did Northamptonshire bowl out for just 33 in a County Championship game at Northampton in 1977?

13 **SIX** Who captained the side from 1967 to 1970?

14 **SIX** Which West Indian bowler, with just 49 wickets, was Northamptonshire's leading wicket-taker in the 1991 Championship season?

15 **THREE** Which Indian Test cricketer made his Northamptonshire debut in 1972?

16   **TWO**   Who was appointed Northamptonshire captain in 1989?

17   **FOUR**   Which batsman, who later became famous for cricket administration, scored 300 for the county versus Surrey at the Oval in 1958?

18   **FOUR**   Which overseas player scored 131 for the county against the Minor Counties East in the 1976 Benson & Hedges Cup at Longton?

19   **SIX**   Which Yorkshire-born cricketer took 7–37 for the county against Worcestershire in the 1984 Nat West Trophy?

20   **FOUR**   Which current first-team opener scored 236 off just 158 balls for the second XI against Worcestershire at Kidderminster in 1989?

21   **SIX**   Which Northamptonshire cricketer took 9–145 in his first Test match for England against Pakistan in 1962?

22   **THREE**   Which West Indian all-rounder scored 234 for Northamptonshire against Gloucestershire in 1986?

23   **FOUR**   Which all-rounder made his Northamptonshire debut against Cambridge University in 1966, aged just 16 years 180 days?

24   **FOUR**   Nigel Felton joined Northamptonshire in 1989, but for which county had he previously played?

25   **THREE**   Which Rhodesian-born all-rounder joined the county in 1991?

SINGLES (11) Northamptonshire lost to Derbyshire in the first Nat West Trophy final in 1981. Name their side.

INNINGS SCORE:

ASHES TESTS II

1 **TWO** Who, in the 4th Test at Adelaide in 1991, scored a hundred on his Test debut against England, to become only the tenth Australian to achieve this feat and the first since Greg Chappell in 1971?

2 **TWO** Who won three consecutive Man of the Match awards during the 1981 Ashes series?

3 **FOUR** Which Australian bowler damaged his right shoulder trying to prevent spectators invading the ground during the 1st Test of the 1982–83 series?

4 **FOUR** Which Australian pace bowler took 41 wickets (av. 12.85) during the 1978–79 series?

5 **SIX** In 1990–91 Jack Russell stumped Dean Jones in the first innings of the Sydney Test. But who was the bowler?

6 **THREE** Which opening batsman hit 175 versus Australia at Leeds in 1985 to register the second highest score by an Englishman on his Ashes debut?

7 **FOUR** (*One run each*) Which four English bowlers have claimed 100 Ashes victims in post-war Tests?

8 **TWO** Who, in the Sydney Test of 1990–91, reached 3000 Test runs against England, a total only exceeded by Sir Don Bradman?

9 **FOUR** Who had his jaw broken by a Bob Willis delivery in the 1977 Centenary Test but bravely returned to bat with his jaw wired up?

10 **THREE** Can you name the Australian skipper who batted on each day of the 1980 Centenary Test at Lord's?

11 **TWO** Which legendary Australian batsman scored 5028 runs (av. 89.78) in 37 Ashes Tests between 1928 and 1948?

12 **THREE** Which Australian pace bowler took the wicket of Phil DeFreitas in the Perth Test in 1991 to claim his 100th Ashes victim in just 17 Tests?

13 **SIX** Which tail-ender added 117 in just 80 minutes with Ian Botham for the eighth wicket during England's famous Headingley win in 1981?

14 **THREE** Which England opener scored 137 in the 6th Test of 1981 to notch up his seventh Ashes ton?

15 **SIX** Which England swing bowler was recruited from the 'A' tour of Sri Lanka to play in the 5th Test of the 1990–91 series only to return immediately after the game?

16 **THREE** Who, in the 1977 Headingley Test, performed a memorable somersault after catching Rod Marsh to secure the Ashes?

17 **FOUR** Which all-rounder, who first toured England in 1948, scored 1511 runs (av. 33.57) and took 87 wickets (av. 22.4) in Ashes cricket?

18 **FOUR** Which Australian pace bowler took 72 minutes, an Australian Test record, to get off the mark in the 1990–91 Sydney Test?

19 **THREE** Which Kent batsman hit 149 versus Australia in the final Test of the 1975 series, reaching his hundred in over six and a half hours?

20 **SIX** Which Warwickshire bowler took 5–42 to help bowl Australia out for 78 in the 200th Ashes Test at Leeds in 1968?

21 **FOUR** Which young Middlesex bowler took 6–77 when England beat Australia by just three runs in the Melbourne Test of 1982–83?

22 **TWO** Who was the England skipper when they lost disastrously by an innings and 85 runs at Edgbaston in 1975?

23 **THREE** Which England spinner was disciplined after the 3rd Test in 1990–91 for kicking the ball at the stumps after having an appeal turned down?

24 **TWO** Who played his 200th Test innings for Australia in the 1990–91 Ashes Test at Brisbane?

25 **FOUR** Which famous batsman captained Australia for the only time in the 2nd Test at Lord's in 1961?

SINGLES (11) Allan Border led the Australians to a resounding series victory in 1989. Name the other 11 players used in the series.

INNINGS SCORE:

AROUND THE COUNTIES

1 **FOUR** (*Two runs each*) Which two left-arm spinners took all 20 wickets for Kent versus Leicestershire at Dartford in 1990?

2 **TWO** Who in 1989 scored the most runs by a batsman in his first County Championship season?

3 **FOUR** Who did champions Essex bowl out for just 51 in their final County Championship game of 1991?

4 **THREE** Name the wicket-keeper who equalled a world record when he took eight catches against Middlesex at Lord's in June 1991.

5 **FOUR** Whose current county ground is on the site of an old racecourse?

6 **THREE** Who in 1990 hit seven hundreds in eight games and broke a world record, but was then released by his county?

7 **FOUR** Wellingborough School shares a distinction with Cheltenham College of being the only school grounds to host first-class cricket. Which county plays at Wellingborough?

8 **SIX** Who in May 1991 was fined £300 by Yorkshire CCC for contesting an umpiring decision?

9 **SIX** For which county did Merv Hughes play one game in the 1983 season?

10 **FOUR** Which Kent player, whose first two scoring shots in first-class cricket were sixes, hit his maiden hundred versus Nottinghamshire at Tunbridge Wells in 1990?

11 **TWO** (*One run each*) Which two former England players did Lancashire release at the end of the 1992 season?

12 **THREE** Which county captain in 1990 published his autobiography entitled *Double Life*, reflecting his career in football and cricket?

13 **FOUR** Whose comments criticising Yorkshire CCC in a national newspaper led to him being dropped from the MCC side to tour Australia in 1958–59?

14 **FOUR** Which Australian pace bowler made one appearance for Lancashire in 1979?

15 **FOUR** Which spinner, after 16 years in the game, scored his first first-class century versus Yorkshire at Worksop in July 1982?

16 **TWO** Which West Indian all-rounder has played for Gloucestershire, Nottinghamshire and Sussex, after starting his career in the Central and Lancashire Leagues?

17 **THREE** Which off-spinner joined Essex in 1990 after previously representing Leicestershire and Nottinghamshire?

18 **SIX** On which county ground would you find the Tom Pearce Stand?

19 **THREE** Yorkshire play matches at Acklam Park. In which industrial town is this ground situated?

20 **FOUR** Who, in his second benefit year with Kent, took 9–59 off 67.5 overs – including 47 maidens – against Warwickshire at Folkestone in 1986?

21 **THREE** Name the wicket-keeper who was instrumental in Essex winning the 1991 County Championship and had previously appeared for Gloucestershire and Leicestershire.

22 **FOUR** Which county play cricket by the seaside at Clarence Park?

23 **THREE** Yorkshire and Lancashire are easily remembered for their white and red rose badges, but which county has the Tudor Rose as its badge?

24 **FOUR** Which all-rounder, born in Johannesburg, scored 10 255 runs (av. 31.45) and took 491 wickets (av. 32.48) in the County Championship for Glamorgan between 1977 and 1989?

25 **FOUR** On which Test ground would you find the Kirkstall Lane End?

SINGLES (7) Up to and including 1992, which seven counties have not won the County Championship outright since the Second World War?

INNINGS SCORE:

PICTURE QUIZ 4

1 **FOUR** Can you name this characteristic English ground? ▼

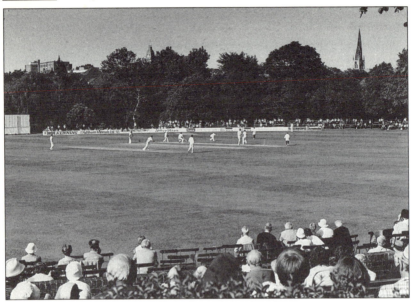

2 **FOUR** Which English Test venue is shown here after rain has stopped play? ▼

3

FOUR Who is this England bowler pictured on the golf course?
◀

4a **TWO** *(One run each)* Name the two England fielders pictured. ▶

4b **TWO** Who is the Australian batsman just about to leave the crease?

4c **FOUR** What happens next?

5 **SINGLES** (17) Name the England team group pictured before the Sydney Test in January 1983.

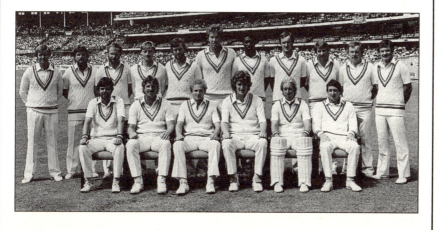

INNINGS SCORE:

41

NOTTINGHAMSHIRE

1   **THREE**   Which left-arm spinner toured Zimbabwe with the England 'A' team in 1989–90?

2   **FOUR**   Which former Cambridge University captain left Lancashire to join Nottinghamshire in 1991, and captained the Trent Bridge outfit before being capped?

3   **FOUR**   Mike Harris joined Nottinghamshire in 1969. But which county did he previously play for?

4   **SIX**   Basharat Hassan played for the county from 1966 to 1985. In which country was he born?

5   **FOUR**   Which South African cricketer was relieved of the county captaincy during the 1979 season when it was revealed he had signed for World Series Cricket?

6   **FOUR**   Eddie Hemmings played for Nottinghamshire from 1979 to 1992. For which county had he previously played?

7   **TWO**   Which famous New Zealand Test cricketer took 105 wickets (av. 14.89) in the 1981 season?

8   **THREE**   Which former England batsman scored 143 not out at Taunton in August 1991 to register his 50th first-class hundred?

9   **FOUR**   Which wicket-keeper made his Nottinghamshire debut in 1976 aged 16 years 287 days?

10   **SIX**   Who took 101 wickets for the county in the 1988 season but was subsequently released in 1992 after a series of injuries?

11   **TWO**   Which opening batsman scored nine centuries for the county in 1990 but was surprisingly released at the end of the 1992 season and rejoined Gloucestershire?

12   **FOUR**   Which former England batsman scored 149 not out for Nottinghamshire versus Devon in the 1988 Nat West Trophy?

13   **THREE**   Which overseas cricketer scored 1018 runs and took 125 wickets in 1988 to become the first cricketer to complete the double since Sir Richard Hadlee in 1984?

14   **SIX**   Which Nottinghamshire batsman scored 635 runs in the 1991 Refuge Assurance League?

15 **TWO** From which county did Nottinghamshire sign England all-rounder Chris Lewis?

16 **THREE** Where did Sir Gary Sobers score 6 sixes in an over in 1968?

17 **FOUR** Which Nottinghamshire and England player scored his maiden first-class century against Derbyshire in 1990, fourteen years after making his debut?

18 **THREE** Which legendary cricketer scored 219 not out for the West Indies *against* Nottinghamshire in 1957 and later appeared *for* the county?

19 **FOUR** Who scored 105* out of a total of 143 versus Hampshire at Bournemouth in 1981, the lowest innings in the history of first-class cricket to contain a hundred?

20 **FOUR** Which famous cricketer took 17–89 for Gloucestershire against Nottinghamshire at Cheltenham back in 1877?

21 **FOUR** Can you name the West Indian wicket-keeper who appeared for Nottinghamshire in the 1960s?

22 **SIX** Which Nottinghamshire batsman gained selection for the 1992 England 'A' tour of West Indies?

23 **SIX** Which famous Australian all-rounder played just one game for Nottinghamshire versus Cambridge University in 1959?

24 **SIX** Name the famous England rugby union full-back who made his Nottinghamshire debut in 1971.

25 **TWO** Which all-rounder was named Man of the Match when Nottinghamshire beat Northamptonshire to win the 1987 Nat West Trophy final?

SINGLES (16) In 1981 Nottinghamshire won the County Championship for the first time in 52 years. Which 16 players represented the county that season?

INNINGS SCORE:

42

ALL-ROUNDERS II

1 **FOUR** Which England all-rounder finished just 67 runs and 13 wickets short of the double in 1984?

2 **FOUR** Which former Worcestershire all-rounder became the ninth man in Test history to be run out for 99 during the 1991–92 Christchurch Test against England?

3 **THREE** Which New Zealand all-rounder joined Nottinghamshire in 1992?

4 **TWO** Which legendary West Indian cricketer scored 1000 runs and took 50 wickets in both the 1962–63 and 1963–64 Sheffield Shield seasons?

5 **FOUR** Name the Yorkshire number eleven who scored 115 not out at Edgbaston in 1982, including a tenth-wicket stand of 149 with Geoffrey Boycott, to record the fourth highest score by a last man in first-class cricket.

6 **THREE** Which Essex and West Indian all-rounder was the first to score 1000 runs and take 100 wickets in one-day cricket in England?

7 **FOUR** Who, at Auckland in 1975, emulated Trevor Bailey and Wilfred Rhodes to become only the third Englishman to score 2000 runs and take 100 wickets in Test matches?

8 **TWO** Who hit 138 in the 1986 Brisbane Ashes Test, including 22 off a Merv Hughes over?

9 **THREE** Which young all-rounder hit 66, batting at number nine, and took 6–96 in Pakistan's famous win against the West Indies at Faisalabad in October 1986?

10 **FOUR** Which famous Australian all-rounder fought as a wartime pilot in Britain?

11 **THREE** Which recently-retired Yorkshire cricketer played football for Manchester United, Huddersfield Town and Halifax Town?

12 **FOUR** Which England off-spinner scored 10 452 runs (av. 26.72) and took 974 wickets (av. 27.60) in County Championship cricket for Yorkshire, Leicestershire and Worcestershire between 1958 and 1981?

13 **FOUR** Which all-rounder was the leading run-getter (518 in 1982–83 and 450 in 1983–84) on the West Indian rebel tours of South Africa?

14 **THREE** Which Australian all-rounder, who had match figures of 7–169 off 58 overs, was Man of the Match as Australia overcame a first-innings deficit of 291 runs to win at Colombo in August 1992?

15 **SIX** Which Essex all-rounder hit 14 off three balls (6.4.4) to clinch victory for England in the Third Test at Christchurch in 1962–63?

16 **SIX** Which former New Zealand skipper played rugby union for England versus Ireland at Dublin in 1946–47?

17 **THREE** Which former England bowler hit a hundred in just 37 minutes for Yorkshire at Edgbaston in 1977?

18 **FOUR** Who was appointed South Africa's first Cricket Manager in August 1992?

19 **FOUR** Which current Northamptonshire player represented Zimbabwe in the 1987 World Cup but will be available for England selection in 1994?

20 **THREE** Which England all-rounder took the wicket of Chris Cairns with his eighth ball in Test cricket during the 1st Test at Christchurch in 1992?

21 **SIX** Who in 1866 won the 440 yards hurdles at the first National Olympians meeting at Crystal Palace, after completing his innings of 244* for England versus Surrey the previous day?

22 **THREE** Which Yorkshire cricketer completed 10 000 first-class runs and 1000 wickets during their draw at the Oval in April 1990?

23 **FOUR** Which Australian opener was Kapil Dev's 400th Test match victim?

24 **FOUR** Which West Indian all-rounder hit 121 off just 127 balls versus England at the Oval in 1973?

25 **FOUR** Which West Indian Test all-rounder did Essex engage to replace Keith Boyce?

SINGLES (10) Excluding Lord Constantine and the Maharajah of Vizianagram, which 10 players have been knighted for their services to cricket?

INNINGS SCORE:

43

MODERN CRICKETING HEROES III

IMRAN KHAN

1 **THREE** With which county did Imran win the 1978 Gillette Cup and the 1986 Nat West Trophy?

2 **FOUR** For whom did Imran score 117* and 106 versus Nottinghamshire in 1974?

3 **THREE** In 1982–83 against India at Faisalabad, Imran became the second player to score a century and take ten wickets in a Test. Who was the first?

4 **SIX** Imran first played for Pakistan in 1971, but who was his first captain?

5 **FOUR** In which year did Imran lead the first Pakistan side to win a Test series in England?

6 **THREE** Imran was named in the Pakistan squad for the first World Cup in 1975, but which former Glamorgan player was Pakistan's skipper?

SUNIL GAVASKAR

7 **THREE** Against which country did Sunil Gavaskar score 774 runs in his first Test rubber in 1970–71?

8 **FOUR** Gavaskar first captained India in their 1978–79 Test series with the West Indies. Who did he replace as skipper?

9 **TWO** Which fast bowler was suspended for knocking Gavaskar over when the Indian attempted a quick single during the 1971 series in England?

10 **THREE** In the 3rd Test versus the West Indies in 1983–84, Gavaskar became the highest ever run scorer in Tests. Whose record did he surpass?

11 **TWO** Who replaced Gavaskar as captain after India lost to Pakistan in 1982–83?

12 **FOUR** On which Test ground did Gavaskar hit 221 in the final Test of the 1979 series?

GREG CHAPPELL

13 **THREE** Who did Chappell ask to bowl underarm to ensure Australia beat New Zealand during a one-day international in 1980–81?

14 **FOUR** During his Test career Chappell held 122 Test catches, to create the record for the most held by an outfielder. Whose record did he beat?

15 **FOUR** (*Two runs each*) For which two Australian state sides did Chappell appear?

16 **THREE** In 1968 Chappell scored 1108 runs and took 26 wickets for which county side?

17 **SIX** What unique record does Chappell share with fellow Australians R A Duff and W H Ponsford?

18 **TWO** In his last Test innings against Pakistan in 1983–84, Chappell scored 182 to pass the record Test aggregate for an Australian. Which legendary batsman previously held the record?

GEOFFREY BOYCOTT

19 **FOUR** (*Two runs each*) Boycott became only the third Yorkshireman to score 100 hundreds; who are the other two?

20 **THREE** Who was Boycott's last England skipper?

21 **TWO** Early in his career Boycott played club cricket for Barnsley. Which TV presenter played alongside him in those days?

22 **THREE** Who did Boycott replace as Yorkshire skipper in 1971?

23 **FOUR** Boycott's best Test match bowling figures are 3–47, but against which country were they achieved?

24 **FOUR** What did Boycott achieve at Delhi on 23 December 1981?

25 **THREE** Against which country did Boycott score most Test runs?

SINGLES (16) During his Test career Geoff Boycott opened the England innings with 16 different partners. Name them.

INNINGS SCORE:

44

SOMERSET

1   **FOUR**   Who in 1990 scored 1559 runs in his debut season for Somerset after leaving Lancashire?

2   **FOUR**   Neil Mallender joined Somerset in 1987, but for which county had he played previously?

3   **THREE**   Which former Kent and England batsman was elected Somerset captain in 1990?

4   **FOUR**   Roland Lefebvre made his Somerset debut in 1990, but for which country has he appeared?

5   **SIX**   Which Australian cricketer, who appeared in the 1983 World Cup, joined Somerset in 1991 but was not classified as an overseas player because he was born in Bradford-on-Avon?

6   **THREE**   Who scored 322 for the county versus Warwickshire at Taunton in 1985?

7   **SIX**   Which recently-retired batsman made his 2nd XI debut in 1969 aged just 13?

8   **TWO**   Which England all-rounder took 100 wickets (av. 16.40) in the 1978 season?

9   **SIX**   Which international cricketer scored 128 not out for Somerset versus Surrey at Brislington in the 1969 John Player League, the first century scored in the competition?

10   **THREE**   Jim Parks joined Somerset in 1973, but for which county had he previously appeared?

11   **THREE**   Who hit 131 for Somerset against Yorkshire, his former county, in the 1974 John Player League?

12   **FOUR**   Name the former Oxford University captain and current newspaper journalist who took 8–17 versus Lancashire at Bath in 1985.

13   **THREE**   Which overseas cricketer scored 2755 runs in the 1991 County Championship?

14   **SIX**   Which England bowler shared in a Somerset record ninth-wicket stand of 183 with Chris Tavare at Hove in 1990?

15 **FOUR** Which overseas bowler took 7–15 for Somerset against Devon at Torquay in the 1990 Nat West Trophy?

16 **SIX** Which Somerset spinner took 9–26 against Lancashire at Weston-super-Mare in 1958?

17 **SIX** Who held 42 catches in 1966 to create a Somerset record for the most catches by an outfielder in a season?

18 **FOUR** Which all-rounder, who is perhaps better known as an umpire, scored 1056 runs and took 114 wickets for the county in 1961?

19 **SIX** Which Australian leg-spinner joined Somerset in 1971?

20 **THREE** Which Somerset cricketer captained England in the one-day internationals against Australia in 1972?

21 **FOUR** Who scored 3019 runs for Somerset in 1961, the last batsman to score 3000 first-class runs in an English season?

22 **THREE** Which New Zealander shared in a third-wicket stand of 319 with Peter Roebuck against Leicestershire at Taunton in 1984?

23 **THREE** Which former Gloucestershire captain joined Somerset for one season in 1991 before moving on to Durham?

24 **SIX** Which Somerset batsman hit 72 sixes in the 1935 season?

25 **SIX** Which left-handed batsman scored two centuries in the match against Gloucestershire at Taunton in 1980?

SINGLES (11) Somerset beat Northamptonshire by 45 runs to win the 1979 Gillette Cup final. Name their side.

INNINGS SCORE:

INTO THE NINETIES

1 **THREE** Which Pakistan Test cricketer was engaged by Somerset for the 1993 season?

2 **TWO** Which county were confirmed as 1992 Sunday League champions after beating Yorkshire on 16 August, the earliest date the competition has been decided?

3 **FOUR** Who in August 1992 scored 119 to record his fourth century in successive Roses matches at Old Trafford?

4 **THREE** Who was reappointed Glamorgan captain for the 1993 season?

5 **FOUR** When David Gower married Thorunn Nash in September 1992, which former England skipper was his best man?

6 **TWO** In May 1992, who was appointed to be Mickey Stewart's successor as England's team boss?

7 **FOUR** (*Two runs each*) Which two non-capped players were selected for England's 1992–93 tour of India?

8 **THREE** Who replaced Andy Lloyd as captain of Warwickshire for the 1993 season?

9 **FOUR** Which company became the first sponsors of 50-overs Sunday League cricket in 1993?

10 **FOUR** What happened to Northamptonshire's captain Allan Lamb when he went out to bat in the 1992 Nat West Trophy final?

11 **TWO** Who in 1992 scored 1000 runs for Derbyshire for the tenth successive season?

12 **THREE** Who was England's oldest player on their 1992–93 tour of India?

13 **FOUR** Which spinner took 23 wickets for Sussex in their last two Championship games of the 1992 season to give them wins over Lancashire and Yorkshire?

14 **SIX** Which two brothers scored centuries for different sides on 2 July 1992?

15   **THREE**   Who did Yorkshire sign in September 1992 to replace Indian prodigy Sachin Tendulkar?

16   **TWO**   Which Australian scored his 24th Test hundred against Sri Lanka at Colombo in September 1992?

17   **SIX**   (*Two runs each*) Which three batsmen hit more than 2000 first-class runs in the 1992 season?

18   **THREE**   Against whom did Zimbabwe make their Test debut at Harare on 18 October 1992?

19   **TWO**   Which English umpire made a record-equalling 48th Test appearance in this match?

20   **TWO**   Which former Lancashire and England player joined Durham for the 1993 season?

21   **FOUR**   Which Australian all-rounder was fined by the Australian Cricket Board for crushing a cigarette packet in a 1992 anti-smoking advertisement?

22   **SIX**   In January 1991, after the England rugby union side had won at Cardiff Arms Park for the first time in 28 years, the England players refused interviews with the media. Which former England cricket captain was acting as their agent?

23   **THREE**   Which former England batsman, who is now a Test match umpire, was appointed Zimbabwe's coach in September 1992?

24   **TWO**   Which side finished bottom of the 1992 Britannic Assurance Championship table?

25   **TWO**   Which famous cricketing personality was an emotional *This is Your Life* subject on 7 October 1992?

SINGLES (11) Uniquely, 11 Nottinghamshire players scored first-class hundreds in 1992. Name them.

INNINGS SCORE:

46

SOUTH AFRICA

1 `FOUR` Which South African batsman scored 356 for South Australia against Western Australia in 1970–71, 325 of which were scored on the first day against an attack including Lillee, McKenzie and Lock?

2 `FOUR` Which spinner, who has a more famous Test-playing brother, took 20 wickets in the 1965 three-match Test series against England?

3 `SIX` Who captained South Africa on their 1965 tour of England?

4 `FOUR` Which Sussex batsman replaced Roland Butcher on the 1990 unofficial tour of South Africa?

5 `FOUR` Who captained South Africa in their 1970–71 Test series against Australia and organised Mike Gatting's rebel tour in 1990?

6 `THREE` Which batsman, who had previously played Test cricket for Australia, scored centuries in both innings against the Australian rebel tourists at Port Elizabeth in February 1987?

7 `FOUR` Who in February 1987 scored 144 in his farewell appearance for South Africa against an Australian rebel XI at Port Elizabeth?

8 `SIX` Which South African Test cricketer hit five consecutive sixes for the South African Fezele XI against Essex at Colchester in 1961?

9 `THREE` Who in April 1992 became the first South African batsman to score a hundred on his Test debut when he hit 163 against the West Indies in Barbados?

10 `THREE` Which prolific opening batsman scored 508 runs in seven Test innings in the 1970 series against Australia, in his only Test match appearances?

11 `TWO` When the 1970 tour of England was cancelled, England played a Rest of the World side for the Guinness Trophy. Who captained the Rest of the World side?

12 `SIX` Prior to South Africa's ban from international cricket, who was the last cricketer to skipper England in a Test match against them?

13   **FOUR**   Who hit 313 not out against Glamorgan at Cardiff in 1990, recording the highest County Championship score by a South African?

14   **TWO**   What is South Africa's domestic competition called?

15   **FOUR**   Which all-rounder, who later appeared for Derbyshire, made the first of his 30 Test match appearances against England in 1964?

16   **FOUR**   Which South African all-rounder hit six consecutive first-class hundreds in 1970–71?

17   **SIX**   Who has taken the most wickets for South Africa in Test matches?

18   **SIX**   Who took nine hours and five minutes to reach his hundred when he scored 105 in the 3rd Test of the 1957–58 series against Australia?

19   **FOUR**   In which city would you be watching cricket at Ellis Park?

20   **SIX**   Which batsman, who later appeared for Derbyshire, scored six centuries for Western Provinces and South African Universities in the 1976–77 season?

21   **SIX**   Who in January 1984 became the youngest player to score a century in South African first-class cricket when he hit 106* for Border versus Natal B at East London?

22   **SIX**   Christopher Dey was dismissed whilst playing for Northern Transvaal against Orange Free State at Bloemfontein in 1973–74, yet he was the non-striker. Why was he given out?

23   **FOUR**   Which Australian tourist took 106 wickets in the 18 matches of their 1957–58 tour of South Africa?

24   **FOUR**   Which former Middlesex player has taken more wickets in first-class matches in South Africa than any other bowler?

25   **THREE**   Which South African pace bowler was named as a Wisden Cricketer of the Year in 1991?

SINGLES (11) In April 1992 South Africa made their return to Test cricket after 22 years. Name their side that faced the West Indies in Barbados.

INNINGS SCORE:

47

SURREY

1   **FOUR**   Who in 1962 scored 2482 runs just one year before his England debut?

2   **THREE**   Who took seven catches in an innings, a record for an outfielder, against Northamptonshire in 1957?

3   **SIX**   Name the Surrey all-rounder who scored 1013 runs and took 104 wickets in 1966, the last double by a Surrey player and the first since Freddie Brown in 1932.

4   **FOUR**   In which country was Pat Pocock born?

5   **FOUR**   Which wicket-keeper, who went on to join Sussex, held 11 catches against Sussex at Hove in 1964 to equal the world record for the most catches in a match?

6   **SIX**   Which former England captain was Waqar Younis' 100th victim of the 1991 season?

7   **FOUR**   Which pace bowler made his England Test debut in 1967 and went on to capture 109 first-class wickets that season?

8   **THREE**   Which Surrey and England batsman, who was highly regarded as a slip fielder, played in goal for Corinthian Casuals and Wimbledon FC?

9   **FOUR**   Who captained Surrey to the 1971 County Championship title?

10   **THREE**   Which spin bowler took seven wickets in 11 balls against Sussex at Eastbourne in 1972?

11   **SIX**   Which Surrey batsman was elected Young Cricketer of the Year in 1972?

12   **SIX**   Name the Surrey and New Zealand cricketer who fielded as a substitute for England against Australia at the Oval in 1972.

13   **FOUR**   Which England batsman shared in a first-wicket stand of 428 with Jack Hobbs against Oxford University at the Oval in 1926?

14   **FOUR**   Which England Test spinner had match figures of 16–83 versus Kent at Blackheath in 1956?

15 **THREE** Graham Clinton joined Surrey in 1979. For which county had he previously played?

16 **FOUR** Against whom did Surrey only score 14 in a County Championship game in 1983?

17 **THREE** Which Surrey captain hit 291 versus Lancashire at the Oval in 1990 to record the fifth highest County Championship score by a Surrey player?

18 **TWO** Which Pakistan bowler made his Surrey debut in 1990 aged just 18?

19 **SIX** Who scored a first-class hundred in just 35 minutes at Northampton in 1920?

20 **FOUR** Which controversial West Indian pace bowler made his Surrey debut in 1979?

21 **THREE** Which Pakistan Test spinner took 6–25 against Derbyshire at the Oval in 1974?

22 **FOUR** In which country was Robin Jackman born?

23 **SIX** Which Pakistan batsman, who went on to play for Worcestershire and Glamorgan, made his Surrey debut in 1965 aged just 17?

24 **THREE** Which Surrey fast bowler was flown out as a replacement for Alan Ward on the 1970–71 tour of Australia?

25 **THREE** Which remarkable batsman scored 43703 runs for the county between 1905 and 1934?

SINGLES (9) Between 1970 and 1992 nine Surrey players represented England at Test level. Name them.

INNINGS SCORE:

48

ENGLAND ON TOUR

1   **THREE**   Which former England captain returned to the England side in Barbados in 1990 whilst working as a journalist there?

2   **TWO**   Which England cricketer, who was run out on 99 at Melbourne in 1979–80, scored his first Test hundred in Australia during the 4th Test in Adelaide in 1990–91?

3   **FOUR**   Name the New Zealand vice-captain who accused Phil Tufnell of 'throwing' at the start of England's 1992 tour of New Zealand.

4   **FOUR**   Which West Indian bowler delivered the ball that broke Graham Gooch's hand in the 3rd Test in Trinidad in 1990?

5   **THREE**   Which England tourist was named International Cricketer of the Year in 1986–87?

6   **FOUR**   Which former England Test cricketer led Western Australia against the MCC in 1970?

7   **TWO**   Which England spinner lost four toes in a motor boat accident during the 1967–68 tour of the West Indies?

8   **FOUR**   Which England pace bowler took career-best figures of 7–74 versus an Australian XI at Hobart in November 1990?

9   **FOUR**   When Mike Brearley broke his arm on the 1977–78 Pakistan tour, which Middlesex colleague replaced him?

10   **THREE**   Name the seam bowler who was placed on stand-by for the 1st Test at Christchurch in 1992 after similarly being drafted in on the 1983–84 tour. (He finally made his England debut in the 1992 series against Pakistan.)

11   **THREE**   Which famous Australian Test bowler made a comeback, aged 42, in England's first tour game against Western Australia in 1990?

12   **SIX**   Which England non-striker was run out by Ewan Chatfield whilst backing up in the 2nd Test at Christchurch in 1977–78?

13   **TWO**   Which former Test cricketer sadly died of a heart attack whilst fulfilling the role of assistant manager on the 1980–81 West Indies tour?

14 **SIX** Ironically, Basil D'Oliveira wasn't originally chosen for the MCC tour of South Africa in 1968–69. Who did he replace?

15 **SIX** Which spin bowler scored 106 in the 3rd unofficial Test for England 'A' against Zimbabwe in 1990, in his only first-class innings of the tour?

16 **TWO** Name the wicket-keeper who was dropped by England for the 4th Test at Adelaide in 1990–91 after 20 consecutive Test appearances.

17 **SIX** Which England batsman holed-in-one at Tollygunge Golf Club during England's 1981–82 tour of India?

18 **THREE** Who was sacked as England captain for the winter tour of West Indies in 1967–68 after he employed delaying tactics in Yorkshire's Championship game with Warwickshire?

19 **FOUR** Which Yorkshire batsman was called up to replace Brian Rose after he had returned home from the 1980–81 West Indies tour with eye problems?

20 **THREE** Which batsman scored 129 not out for England in the one-day international at Port of Spain on 4 March 1986?

21 **FOUR** Which future England skipper toured South Africa in 1964–65 and scored just 406 runs in 19 innings (av. 25.37)?

22 **SIX** Name the assistant manager who played in the 3rd unofficial Test against Sri Lanka in 1985–86 because of a shortage of spinners in the England squad.

23 **FOUR** Which Middlesex opening batsman was summoned to the West Indies for the 1986 tour after captain Mike Gatting had his nose broken?

24 **FOUR** Which former Essex batsman managed England's tour of Australia in 1982–83?

25 **TWO** Who joined the England party for their 1992 New Zealand tour after appearing in pantomime in Bournemouth?

SINGLES (11) Name the England side that played in the 1977 Centenary Test match at Melbourne.

INNINGS SCORE:

49

BOWLERS II

1   **FOUR**   Who took 8–148 in the 1985 Old Trafford Test and was the only Australian to take a wicket in England's total of 482–9 declared?

2   **FOUR**   Which England pace bowler was offered a contract to play rugby league in 1985–86 but turned it down?

3   **SIX**   Which England seam bowler delivered 35 consecutive overs against Pakistan at Headingley in 1982?

4   **TWO**   Name the Kent, Worcestershire and England bowler who announced his retirement at the end of the 1992 season.

5   **THREE**   Name the giant Kent bowler who was born in Northern Ireland, brought up in Australia, but is available for England selection.

6   **THREE**   Which Pakistan bowler took the most wickets on their 1992 tour of England?

7   **THREE**   Who took 5–26 for Lancashire against Northamptonshire in the 1990 Nat West final to earn himself the Man of the Match award?

8   **SIX**   Which South African pace bowler appeared for Somerset in 1992?

9   **FOUR**   Peter Robinson (on 27 August 1970) and Phil DeFreitas (3 August 1991) were the first and 1000th first-class wickets for which spin bowler?

10   **SIX**   Which former Essex all-rounder took his 200th wicket for Cambridgeshire on 22 July 1991 after just 37 minor county appearances?

11   **TWO**   Which Australian pace bowler was originally selected as Yorkshire's first overseas player before injury forced him to pull out of his contract?

12   **THREE**   Which overseas bowler took 8–26 for Essex at Old Trafford in 1971 to record what are still the best ever figures in the history of the Sunday League?

13   **TWO**   Which right-arm fast bowler made his Test debut at Leeds in 1952 and helped reduce the Indians to 0 for 4 wickets?

14   **SIX**   Which bowler, who was playing for Fleetwood in the Northern League, was recruited to play for Australia in the 1981 Ashes series despite only having played in six first-class games?

15   **FOUR**   Which England spin bowler took five wickets against Sri Lanka in the 1983 World Cup?

16   **THREE**   Neal Radford was named as one of the Wisden Cricketers of the Year in 1985, his debut season for Worcestershire. From which county did Radford join the New Road outfit?

17   **FOUR**   Which England swing bowler took 10–104 versus Australia at Edgbaston in 1985?

18   **THREE**   Which Pakistan all-rounder took hat-tricks in two Sharjah Tournament games in 1989–90?

19   **FOUR**   Which West Indian bowler was taken on the 1978–79 Indian tour despite only one first-class appearance for Barbados?

20   **THREE**   Which former coal worker took 11 wickets (av. 18.72) on the 1982 English rebel tour of South Africa and made his Test debut in 1985 after serving his three-year ban?

21   **TWO**   Which West Indian bowler took 119 wickets (av. 13.62) for Hampshire in 1974?

22   **FOUR**   Which young Australian pace bowler made his Test debut versus Pakistan in 1972–73, but only discovered after the match that he had played with a broken bone in his foot?

23   **THREE**   Who in 1991 became Damon Welch's famous father-in-law?

24   **FOUR**   Which Yorkshire bowler made his first-class debut in 1981, aged just 16 years, 2 months and 13 days?

25   **THREE**   Which was the only side to dismiss New Zealand's Martin Crowe in the 1992 World Cup?

SINGLES (7) Which seven bowlers took over 200 Test wickets in the 1980s?

INNINGS SCORE:

50

SUSSEX

1   **SIX**   Who took 10–49 versus Warwickshire at Worthing in 1964, the last occasion a bowler took 10 first-class wickets in an innings in this country?

2   **THREE**   At which ground will you find the 'Tate Gates'?

3   **FOUR**   Which famous all-rounder scored 156 versus Lancashire at Hove in 1967 on his County Championship debut?

4   **SIX**   Which batsman, the last white West Indian Test cricketer, scored 1305 runs for the county in 1970?

5   **THREE**   Which former Sussex and England player has the middle name of Augustine?

6   **FOUR**   Which South African Test batsman hit 254 versus Middlesex at Hove in 1980?

7   **THREE**   Which former Sussex captain stood for Parliament against James Callaghan at Cardiff South East in the 1964 General Election?

8   **SIX**   Who played in 423 consecutive Championship games for Sussex between August 1954 and July 1969?

9   **FOUR**   Which recent Sussex captain was born in Germany and had a middle name of Troutbeck?

10   **FOUR**   Which batsman scored 34152 runs for the county between 1928 and 1955?

11   **THREE**   Which Sussex player was elected Young Cricketer of the Year in 1979?

12   **SIX**   Which England Test cricketer took a hat-trick in 1978 to gain his first ever wickets in first-class cricket?

13   **FOUR**   Which Sussex all-rounder played in two Tests against Pakistan in 1982?

14   **FOUR**   Can you name the Australian Test cricketer who took 6–9 against Ireland at Downpatrick in the 1990 Nat West Trophy?

15   **FOUR**   Who scored 1604 runs for Sussex in 1985, his last season before joining a Northern county?

16   **THREE**   Which Sussex wicket-keeper was chosen for the 1982–83 tour of Australia?

17   **FOUR**   Which batsman, who toured South Africa in 1990 with the England rebel side, was made captain of Sussex in 1992?

18   **THREE**   John Snow played the majority of his cricket for Sussex. But he made a comeback playing limited-overs cricket, primarily as a batsman, for which county?

19   **TWO**   Which young Sussex leg-spinner was chosen to represent an England XI against a Rest of the World XI in July-August 1991 and gained full Test recognition a year later?

20   **FOUR**   Imran Khan joined Sussex by special registration in 1977, but from which county?

21   **FOUR**   Which South African bowler took 81 wickets in 1981?

22   **THREE**   In which seaside resort would you find the 'Saffrons'?

23   **.FOUR**   Who, aged just 20, hit four Championship centuries for Sussex in the 1992 season and was subsequently chosen to tour Australia with the England 'A' squad?

24   **SIX**   Which bird can be found on the Sussex badge?

25   **THREE**   Which Durham University graduate, and occasional wicket-keeper, scored five first-class hundreds for Sussex in 1992?

SINGLES (11) Sussex lost to Lancashire in the 1970 Gillette Cup final. Name their side.

INNINGS SCORE:

PICTURE QUIZ 5

1 **FOUR** Where is this county ground? ▼

2 **FOUR** Identify this English Test match arena. ▼

3   **FOUR** Who is this England cricketer relaxing whilst surfing?

4a   **FOUR** What has just happened?

4b   **FOUR** *(Two runs each)* Name the two sides involved.

5   **TEN** *(Two runs each)* Name the five England tourists enjoying a splash after the 1990 Test match at Guyana had been washed out. ▼

INNINGS SCORE:

51

ENGLISH TEST CRICKET II

1   **THREE**   Which wicket-keeper was the second Cornishman, after Jack Crapp, to play for England?

2   **FOUR**   Mike Brearley captained England in 31 Tests, losing only four. Which side beat England on all four occasions?

3   **FOUR**   Which pace bowler made his Test debut versus New Zealand at Lord's in 1983 after just 19 first-class matches?

4   **TWO**   Which England fast bowler presented Yorkshire Television's 'Indoor League'?

5   **SIX**   (*Two runs each*) Name the three Cheshire-born bowlers who spearheaded England's attack against Australia in the 4th Test at Old Trafford in 1985.

6   **FOUR**   Which England spinner took the wicket of Bruce Edgar with his fourth ball in Test cricket at Lord's in 1978?

7   **THREE**   At which English Test venue would you find the 'Sydney Barnes Wicket Gate'?

8   **THREE**   Which England batsman, who made his Test debut back in 1978, scored his first home Test hundred against Australia at Old Trafford in 1985?

9   **TWO**   Which English cricketer published a book entitled *A Cricketer's Art* in 1988?

10   **TWO**   On 19 July 1952, England bowled out a Test side twice. Name their fragile opposition.

11   **THREE**   Which England all-rounder appeared as an extra in the film *Chariots of Fire*?

12   **FOUR**   Which Englishman made his Test debut at Lord's in 1975 aged 34, scored 50 and 45, and also captured Ashley Mallett's wicket with his fourth ball?

13   **THREE**   (*One run each*) Which three cricketers, who had served Test bans for playing on the 1990 unofficial South African tour, were selected for England's 1992–93 tour of India?

14   **SIX**   Which Kent and England wicket-keeper hit 123 before lunch against South Africa at the Oval in August 1935?

15 **FOUR** Which batsman had his left arm broken by a Winston Davis delivery at Old Trafford in 1984, but bravely returned to bat with his arm in a sling to ensure that Allan Lamb reached his hundred?

16 **SIX** Which medium-paced bowler was recalled by England for the 1963 West Indian series after an 11 year absence?

17 **FOUR** Which Warwickshire batsman became the first England player to be run out twice in the same Test when he was dismissed in that manner against India at the Oval in 1971?

18 **THREE** Who, at Port of Spain in 1967–68, scored 143 to claim his fourth hundred in successive Tests and surpass Sir Len Hutton's record of 52 Test match fifties?

19 **THREE** Who, at Auckland in 1987–88, became the ninth Englishman (and the fourth Yorkshireman) to be dismissed in a Test for 99?

20 **FOUR** Which former England captain wrote the book *Double Century*, a bicentenary history of MCC?

21 **TWO** Which Lancashire pace bowler concluded England's victory in the 1971 Leeds Test versus Pakistan with three wickets in four balls?

22 **FOUR** Sir Len Hutton's son went on to play for Yorkshire and England. What's his christian name?

23 **SIX** Which England player batted on all five days of the 1984 Lord's Test against the West Indies?

24 **THREE** Which former England bowler was named as Nottinghamshire's Cricket Manager in 1992?

25 **FOUR** Which 43-year-old former England spinner took over 100 wickets for Warwickshire in the 1983 season?

SINGLES (15) Name the 15 Englishmen who toured South Africa on the 1981–82 rebel tour.

INNINGS SCORE:

52

ENGLAND TEST CAPTAINS

1   **FOUR**   Which England skipper hit 152 at Faisalabad in 1983–84 to become the first England captain to score a hundred since Tony Greig in 1976–77?

2   **SIX**   Name the all-rounder who in 1980–81 replaced Ian Botham as skipper on the second day of the Port of Spain Test when Botham went off with a hand injury.

3   **TWO**   Which former England captain was a violinist in the Welsh National Youth Orchestra?

4   **THREE**   Which former England skipper was appointed Chairman of Yorkshire CC in 1981?

5   **FOUR**   Which England skipper hit 1294 runs in June and 1050 runs in August of 1949?

6   **THREE**   Who was the first England skipper to score 100 first-class hundreds?

7   **FOUR**   (*Two runs each*) When Colin Cowdrey was married in September 1956, both his best man and the vicar officiating had led the England side. Name them.

8   **THREE**   Which England captain was once reported to have said, "As far as I was concerned, there were a few people singing and dancing and that was that"?

9   **TWO**   Which England skipper of the 1980s often used tapes to hypnotise himself before play?

10   **SIX**   Which future skipper toured the West Indies with the England Youth side in 1972, primarily as reserve wicket-keeper to Gloucestershire's Andy Stovold?

11   **THREE**   Which future captain finished top of the 1964 Civil Service examinations?

12   **FOUR**   Which England captain scored 138 in the 1st Test against South Africa at Leeds in 1951?

13   **THREE**   Geoffrey Boycott was dismissed seven times in Test matches by which Australian bowler?

14 **TWO** Who led England on the infamous 1932–33 'Bodyline Tour'?

15 **FOUR** Who, at Bridgetown in 1990, scored a hundred in his first match as England captain?

16 **SIX** Which former England skipper was appointed Chairman of the TCCB in 1985?

17 **THREE** Who was the first England captain to score 3000 runs and take 100 wickets in an England career?

18 **FOUR** Which former England captain was released by Kent (in 1991) and by Glamorgan (in 1992)?

19 **FOUR** Which famous batsman deputised as captain during the Old Trafford Test against Australia in 1926, but never led the side again in 61 Test appearances?

20 **TWO** Which pace bowler was appointed to lead England for the first time in the 1982 home series against India?

21 **SIX** Which England Test captain won an Olympic boxing medal at middleweight in 1908?

22 **THREE** Who replaced Sir Colin Cowdrey as skipper when the Kent player tore an achilles tendon just before the 1969 series against the West Indies?

23 **FOUR** Which England captain won nine successive Test match tosses (2 v West Indies in 1959–60, 5 v South Africa in 1960 and 2 v Australia in 1961) at cumulative odds of 512–1?

24 **THREE** Who was selected to lead the England 'A' tour to the West Indies in 1992 but had to return home early due to a hand injury?

25 **FOUR** Which Middlesex cricketer was Sir Colin Cowdrey's vice-captain on England's 1967–68 tour of the West Indies?

SINGLES (10) Which ten England captains were not born in Great Britain?

INNINGS SCORE:

53

GILLETTE CUP/ NAT WEST TROPHY

1 **THREE** During the existence of the Gillette Cup (1963–80) which team played in the most matches?

2 **FOUR** Which overseas batsman hit 206 and took six wickets for Warwickshire against Oxfordshire in 1984?

3 **THREE** Name the former England batsman who led Cheshire to victory over Northamptonshire in the 1988 Nat West Trophy.

4 **TWO** Which Essex and England batsman became the first to score a hundred in the Nat West Trophy when he hit 101 versus Hertfordshire at Hitchin in 1981?

5 **FOUR** Which team won the last Gillette Cup final, beating Surrey by eight wickets in 1980?

6 **SIX** Which minor county side defeated Glamorgan at Swansea in 1974?

7 **THREE** Which spin bowler helped Mike Garnham to hit 14 off Mike Atherton's last over in the memorable Essex-Lancashire second round game in 1992?

8 **SIX** Which team defeated Sussex by 4 wickets in 1968 to win the Gillette Cup for the second time?

9 **THREE** Which current Somerset bowler took 7–37 for Northamptonshire against Worcestershire at Northampton in 1984?

10 **TWO** Which famous Sussex all-rounder hit 608 runs (av. 24.32) and took 47 wickets (av. 19.44) in the competition between 1967 and 1978?

11 **FOUR** On 20 October 1980, a dinner was held at London's Savoy Hotel to commemorate Gillette's sponsorship of the event. Who was named by them as 'Man of the Series'?

12 **TWO** Which former Kent and England batsman hit 162 not out for Somerset against Devon at Torquay in 1990?

13 **SIX** (*Two runs each*) From the Somerset side that lost the 1967 Gillette Cup final, name the three players who went on to be Test match umpires.

14 **THREE** In 1973 Durham became the first minor county to beat a county side in the Gillette Cup. Which side lost to them?

15 **FOUR** Which Gloucestershire and Pakistan opener hit 111 versus Leicestershire and 122 versus Lancashire in the 1975 Gillette Cup competition?

16 **THREE** Which overseas bowler took 4–7 and claimed the Man of the Match award when Northamptonshire thrashed Yorkshire by 133 runs at Northampton in July 1992?

17 **SIX** (*One run each*) Which six cricketers won five or more 'Man of the Match' awards in Gillette Cup history (1963–80)?

18 **TWO** Which wicket-keeper made six dismissals for Derbyshire against Essex at Derby in 1981?

19 **THREE** Which bowler took 6–15 against Somerset at Taunton to help Yorkshire reach Lord's for their 1965 Gillette Cup success?

20 **FOUR** Surrey lost the 1991 final to Hampshire by four wickets. But how did they beat Oxfordshire in an earlier round?

21 **FOUR** Which Sussex opener hit 119 versus Glamorgan and 141 not out versus Warwickshire in the 1980 competition?

22 **SIX** Which Indian spinner helped Hertfordshire to their shock 1976 Gillette Cup win over Essex, making them the first minor county side to reach the quarter-finals of the competition?

23 **FOUR** When the sponsorship of the Gillette Cup ended in 1980, which West Indian batsman had hit the highest score in the history of the competition, 177 versus Glamorgan in 1977?

24 **TWO** Which former England bowler took 7–19 for Worcestershire in their 1991 Nat West Trophy game against Bedfordshire?

25 **THREE** Which county appeared in their first ever one-day final when they faced Middlesex in the 1977 Gillette Cup final?

SINGLES (11) Despite Geoffrey Boycott being unfit for the 1969 final, Yorkshire still managed to beat Derbyshire. Name the Yorkshire eleven.

INNINGS SCORE:

54

WARWICKSHIRE

1 **FOUR** Test cricketer Bob Barber joined Warwickshire in 1963, but which county had he previously captained.

2 **FOUR** Who, with 1368 runs, was Warwickshire's top run-getter in the 1992 County Championship?

3 **SIX** Who in 1963 threw off his gloves to take a hat-trick against Essex at Clacton?

4 **SIX** (*Two runs each*) Despite a highly successful 1991 County Championship season, only three Warwickshire batsman scored hundreds in the competition. Name them.

5 **FOUR** Which West Indian cricketer scored 253 versus Nottinghamshire at Trent Bridge in 1968, sharing in a stand of 402 with Khalid Ibadulla?

6 **SIX** In which country was Dermot Reeve born?

7 **THREE** Which England batsman scored 3245 runs during the 1959 season, including 1209 in July alone?

8 **SIX** Who in 1971 won the Young Player of the Year award?

9 **THREE** Which side defeated Warwickshire in the 1992 Nat West semi-finals?

10 **FOUR** Which former England batsman became Warwickshire skipper in 1988?

11 **THREE** Prior to making his England Test debut, Gladstone Small had played for which Australian state side?

12 **FOUR** Which Warwickshire all-rounder, who took a hat-trick in the 1989 season, repeated the feat against Sussex in 1990 using Ted Munton's shoes which were two sizes too large?

13 **SIX** Roger Twose made his Warwickshire debut in 1989. Name his famous uncle who kept wicket for England.

14 **TWO** Which South African bowler, with 74 victims, took the most Championship wickets for Warwickshire in the 1992 season?

15   **THREE** In Warwickshire's memorable 1982 Championship game at Southport, Gladstone Small was called up on Test stand-by. Name the Warwickshire manager who replaced him and became the first substitute to take a wicket in first-class cricket.

16   **TWO** Which England pace bowler and future England skipper took 7–32 against Yorkshire in the 1981 Benson & Hedges Cup?

17   **SIX** Where was the Warwickshire and England batsman John Jameson born?

18   **FOUR** Which former England bowler captained the side from 1975–77?

19   **SIX** Which former Warwickshire all-rounder once fought for the South African heavyweight boxing title?

20   **THREE** Which former Yorkshire and England bowler joined Warwickshire in 1983?

21   **FOUR** Who scored 254 at Southport in 1982 to record the fourth highest Warwickshire score in County Championship history?

22   **THREE** Who in 1972 was banned from playing first-class cricket until 1 July, but then took 8–44 (including a hat-trick) in the last game of the season?

23   **FOUR** Mike Smith joined the county in 1956, but for which side had he previously played?

24   **FOUR** Who in 1986 hit his 100th hundred versus Lancashire at Edgbaston?

25   **THREE** Which England pace bowler bowled an 18-ball over, including 11 no-balls, versus Middlesex in August 1982?

SINGLES (17) When Warwickshire won the 1972 County Championship, which 17 players were used?

INNINGS SCORE:

55

CLAIM TO FAME

1 **THREE** Who, at Old Trafford in 1983, plundered a century against the docile bowling of David Gower and James Whitaker in just 35 minutes?

2 **TWO** Which cricketer played in *Jack and the Beanstalk* at the Alhambra Theatre, Bradford in 1990?

3 **FOUR** On which English Test ground did Simply Red perform in 1992?

4 **THREE** Glenn Turner's brother Greg is a professional in which sport?

5 **FOUR** Name the Lancashire and Worcestershire cricketer who played in goal for Aston Villa in the 1974–75 League Cup final.

6 **FOUR** Which famous *Sunday Times* journalist took 9–46 for Sussex versus Lancashire at Hove in 1955?

7 **FOUR** Which Gloucestershire and Zimbabwe all-rounder became the first to take a hat-trick and score a half-century in a Sunday League game at Edgbaston in 1989?

8 **SIX** Which Australian bowler took 5–63 in England's first innings of the 1977 Oval Test?

9 **THREE** Which FA Premier League goalkeeper played in the Shropshire side that beat Yorkshire in the 1984 Nat West Trophy?

10 **FOUR** (*Two runs each*) At Madras in 1984–85, which two batsmen became the first two Englishmen to score double centuries in the same Test innings?

11 **THREE** Which Australian batsman hit 137 and 107 for Victoria versus South Australia at Adelaide in 1982–83? (The latter was reached in just 43 minutes off 34 balls).

12 **FOUR** Which famous cricketer helped form the English Bowling Association in 1903?

13 **SIX** In 1978 Brian McKechnie kicked the winning penalty for the All Blacks against Wales, but on 1 February 1981 he was involved in which famous cricketing incident?

14   **THREE**   Which Englishman hit 148 in Durban in 1964–65 to become the first player to score centuries in seven different Test-playing countries?

15   **TWO**   On which English Test match ground would you find 'Old Father Time'?

16   **SIX**   Which Australian took a catch with his first touch of the ball on his Test debut versus New Zealand at Brisbane in 1987–88?

17   **THREE**   Which former England captain has won the President's Putter golf tournament?

18   **TWO**   Which former West Indian wicket-keeper was acting as match referee when the match ball was changed in the 4th one-day international (England v Pakistan) at Lord's in 1992?

19   **SIX**   Which England wicket-keeper won £1000 on the ITV quiz show *Double Your Money* answering questions on jewellery? (He promptly gave half to Rev. David Sheppard's Islington Boys Club and kept the other half)

20   **TWO**   Which England skipper changed his middle name to Dylan as a mark of respect to rock star Bob Dylan?

21   **SIX**   Which bowler, who was the first Anglo-Indian to play for India, took the valuable wicket of Clive Lloyd in the 1983 World Cup final?

22   **THREE**   Australian wicket-keeper Rodney Marsh has a golf-playing brother. What's his brother's christian name?

23   **TWO**   Against which country, in September 1985, did Sri Lanka gain their first ever Test victory?

24   **FOUR**   What was unusual about the Australian side named to face the West Indies in the 3rd Test at Port of Spain in 1991?

25   **THREE**   Which Australian batsman reportedly consumed 58 cans of beer on the plane flight from Sydney to London in 1989, to break Rodney Marsh's unofficial record of 50 cans?

SINGLES (11) Which 11 England players faced Sri Lanka at Colombo in 1981–82 in the first Test between the nations?

INNINGS SCORE:

56

MOVING COUNTIES

1   **SIX**   Which batsman scored 157 for Essex against Glamorgan at Cardiff in 1991, then left the county to join Worcestershire at the end of the season?

2   **THREE**   Which former England batsman, who averaged over 40 in first-class cricket for Gloucestershire, refused to sign a further contract with the county at the end of the 1992 season?

3   **FOUR**   With which county did David Smith start his county career back in 1973?

4   **SIX**   Which pace bowler spent six seasons with Hampshire before joining Essex in 1990?

5   **THREE**   Which England batsman, released by Surrey at the end of the 1986 season, then joined Glamorgan and enjoyed immense success, including being the first English-qualified batsman to 1000 runs in 1989 and 1990?

6   **FOUR**   (*Two runs each*) For which two counties has West Indian pace bowler Anthony Merrick appeared?

7   **TWO**   Which England batsman joined Hampshire from Leicestershire in 1990?

8   **THREE**   Which England all-rounder joined Lancashire from Leicestershire at the end of the 1988 season?

9   **FOUR**   (*Two runs each*) For which two counties has West Indian all-rounder Eldine Baptiste appeared?

10   **SIX**   Left-arm bowler Paul Taylor was a revelation for Northamptonshire in 1992, but for which county did he appear between 1984 and 1986 with much less success?

11   **FOUR**   In 1992 Leicestershire bowler David Millns took more than 50 first-class wickets for the second successive season. But for which side did he appear in 1988 and 1989?

12   **THREE**   England fast bowler Ken Shuttleworth left Old Trafford in 1975. For which county did he reappear in 1977?

13   **FOUR**   Who in 1988 was banned from playing county cricket for ten weeks and fined £2000 for a supposed breach of contract when he signed for Derbyshire whilst still under contract with Glamorgan?

14 **THREE** Apart from Yorkshire, which other county did umpire Dickie Bird play for?

15 **FOUR** Coach Alan Ormrod was dismissed by Lancashire in August 1992, but from which county did he join the Old Trafford outfit back in 1984?

16 **FOUR** Which Yorkshire batsman, who represented England in three one-day internationals, hit 9657 County Championship runs between 1975 and 1989 before leaving the county?

17 **TWO** Which Pakistan batsman hit 227 for Sussex 2nd XI against Hampshire at Hove in 1975 whilst qualifying to represent the county?

18 **FOUR** Which Kent batsman, who has since played for Gloucestershire, hit 234 versus Middlesex at Canterbury in 1990 to record the third highest post-war score for the county?

19 **THREE** Which all-rounder, who also went on to represent Surrey and Lancashire, hit 12891 runs (av. 29.23) and took 451 wickets (28.17) in County Championship cricket for Hampshire before leaving the county in 1984?

20 **SIX** Which left-arm spin bowler moved from Lancashire to Worcestershire in 1955, and from Worcestershire to Derbyshire in 1959, becoming the first player to be capped by three different counties?

21 **TWO** Which England spinner left Leicestershire at the end of the 1986 season to join Northamptonshire and played against his old side in the 1992 Nat West Trophy final?

22 **THREE** Which seam bowler, who is nicknamed 'Godber' and 'Norman Stanley' after the BBC TV series *Porridge*, left Yorkshire to join Lancashire for the 1992 season?

23 **SIX** From which county did Hampshire engage the services of slow bowler Rajesh Maju in 1984?

24 **FOUR** Which off-spinner left Hampshire for Glamorgan in 1989 but was unable to fulfil his contract because of injury?

25 **FOUR** (*Two runs each*) For which two counties has West Indian bowler Winston Davis played?

SINGLES (6) In 1971, before Chelmsford became their base, Essex played home matches at which six venues?

INNINGS SCORE:

57

WEST INDIES

1. **FOUR** When Alan Knott broke the record for the number of Test dismissals, at the Oval in 1976, which former Glamorgan batsman was his 219th victim?

2. **FOUR** Who was the first Antiguan to play Test cricket?

3. **THREE** Who, at Wellington in February 1981, became the second West Indian to take 250 Test wickets when he dismissed Jeff Crowe?

4. **THREE** Who, at Old Trafford in 1976, hit 134 out of an innings total of 211, a percentage (63.5%) previously bettered only by Bannermann in the very first Test match?

5. **FOUR** Who, at Birmingham in 1957, bowled 98 overs (588 balls) in an innings against England?

6. **THREE** Who, at Swansea in 1976, scored 201 in just 120 minutes, the fastest double century in history?

7. **THREE** Phil Simmons, a West Indian tourist in 1988, needed an emergency operation after being hit on the head by which English fast bowler?

8. **TWO** Who was the first West Indian to score 100 first-class hundreds?

9. **FOUR** Which West Indian pace bowler, who is a qualified airline pilot, joined Lancashire in 1978?

10. **THREE** Which Surrey and West Indies fast bowler hit three successive sixes off Pakistan's Mohammed Nazir at Faisalabad on 11 December 1980, his 26th birthday?

11. **SIX** When Mike Denness' side beat the West Indies at Port of Spain in 1974, which home batsman got a pair?

12. **THREE** Who was the first West Indian who had received a life ban for touring South Africa to be re-selected for his country?

13. **FOUR** Sir Gary Sobers scored 163 not out versus England in Jamaica in 1966. Can you name his cousin who helped him put on 274 for the sixth wicket?

14. **SIX** Who made his West Indies debut against England at Headingley in 1988 after Gordon Greenidge had pulled out injured?

15 **TWO** Which pace bowler took 14 England wickets in the 5th Test at the Oval in 1976?

16 **FOUR** When Sir Gary Sobers scored his Test record 365 not out, which West Indian scored 260 not out in the same innings?

17 **THREE** In 1963 Sobers topped the English first-class batting averages. Which other tourist topped the bowling averages?

18 **SIX** Viv Richards retired from Test cricket in 1991 after scoring over 8000 Test runs. But which pace bowler dismissed him on the most occasions (nine)?

19 **TWO** Name the West Indian who was the first batsman to reach 8000 Test runs.

20 **FOUR** Which batsman scored a hundred at Brisbane in 1975, his 23rd Test appearance, to complete centuries against all the Test-playing nations?

21 **SIX** Which West Indian bowler took 32 wickets in the 1974–75 Test series against India?

22 **SIX** Which batsman, on his Test debut, bowled the final over of the 1991 Oval Test and took the wicket of Mark Ramprakash with his third ball?

23 **TWO** Who did the West Indies beat in the first World Cup final in 1975?

24 **SIX** Which West Indian was the first batsman to make nine Test scores in the nineties?

25 **FOUR** Which former West Indies captain was shot dead in September 1989 after disturbing burglars in his Trinidad home?

SINGLES (16) Name the 16 players originally selected by the West Indies for their 1991 England tour.

INNINGS SCORE:

58

WORCESTERSHIRE

1 **FOUR** Which former Aston Villa goalkeeper joined Worcestershire in 1972?

2 **FOUR** Which West Indian Test cricketer took 6–33 for Worcestershire against Middlesex at Lord's in the 1972 John Player League?

3 **THREE** Which New Zealand batsman scored 311 not out for the county against Warwickshire at Worcester in 1982?

4 **SIX** Which recent Worcestershire player has a degree in Russian?

5 **THREE** Which batsman, a former county captain, scored 34 490 runs for Worcestershire between 1946 and 1967?

6 **FOUR** Which overseas cricketer made his Worcestershire debut against the touring Indians in 1971, aged just 18?

7 **SIX** Name the former Shrewsbury and Sheffield United wing-half who made his Worcestershire debut in 1963.

8 **FOUR** Which all-rounder, a famous England Test player, received the MBE in the 1969 Birthday Honours List?

9 **SIX** Who in 1964 won an FA Cup winners medal for West Ham and took 64 wickets for Worcestershire to top the first-class averages?

10 **SIX** Which Worcestershire cricketer, who made his Test debut in 1961, took 171 first-class wickets that summer?

11 **THREE** Which bowler, a former Lancashire cricketer, took 101 wickets for Worcestershire in 1985?

12 **SIX** Which all-rounder, who later played Test cricket for New Zealand, put on 227 for the sixth wicket with Ted Hemsley at the Parks in 1976?

13 **TWO** Who took over the Worcestershire captaincy from Phil Neale at the end of the 1991 season?

14 **TWO** Who scored 1000 runs before the end of May in 1988?

15 **FOUR** Who hit 100 not out and was named Man of the Match in the 1991 Refuge Assurance Cup final?

16 **FOUR** Against which county did Graeme Hick score 405 not out in 1988?

17 **TWO** Which Australian Test cricketer joined Worcestershire in 1991 and scored four Sunday League hundreds that season?

18 **FOUR** Which wicket-keeper, a former Yorkshire cricketer, had 65 first-class victims in 1990, more than any other keeper?

19 **THREE** Who scored 160 off only 111 balls against Kent in the 1991 Sunday League?

20 **SIX** Which Worcestershire pace bowler took 6–26 against Surrey in the 1974 John Player League?

21 **FOUR** Which spin bowler, who made his Test debut in 1964, was appointed county captain in 1971?

22 **FOUR** Who in 1991 scored 237 versus Oxford University, 157 of which were scored before lunch?

23 **THREE** Worcestershire won the County Championship for the first time in 1964, but who captained the side?

24 **SIX** Who in July 1991 stepped in to replace Ian Botham in the match against Kent at Worcester, causing speculation that the all-rounder was leaving the county?

25 **FOUR** Which West Indian all-rounder took a hat-trick against Middlesex at Lord's in 1981?

SINGLES (11) In 1991 Worcestershire finally won a one-day final at Lord's. Which 11 players represented the county in their Benson & Hedges Cup final win over Lancashire?

INNINGS SCORE:

59

MIXED BAG

1 **THREE** Who in 1972 became the second Scot to captain a county?

2 **TWO** Which England captain claimed he would make the West Indies 'grovel' in 1976?

3 **THREE** Who succeeded Arthur Wrigley as BBC Radio's scorer in 1966?

4 **FOUR** Which cricketer captained Yorkshire to an innings win over the touring Australians in 1968 when regular skipper Brian Close was absent?

5 **TWO** Who played for Essex against Surrey at the Oval on 30 August 1988 after batting for England against Sri Lanka at Lord's the same day?

6 **FOUR** Who, at Perth in 1982, became the 500th cricketer and first black Jamaican to represent England in Test matches?

7 **FOUR** Why was play held up during the 1973 Lord's Test between England and the West Indies?

8 **SIX** What was unusual about Dennis Lillee's dismissal in the 1st Test at Perth in 1979?

9 **TWO** Which Indian cricketer made his 115th Test appearance, beating Sir Colin Cowdrey's record, at Edgbaston in 1986?

10 **FOUR** Who has scored the most runs for either Oxford or Cambridge University?

11 **FOUR** (*Two runs each*) When Colin Cowdrey and Bill Lawry were unfit, which two cricketers captained England and Australia in the 4th Test at Headingley in 1968?

12 **THREE** Which former England all-rounder, who is a member of the BBC's *Test Match Special* team, won an FA Amateur Cup medal with Walthamstow?

13 **FOUR** Which England cricketer did Peter Roebuck once describe as, 'a scowling, splay-footed, unshaven youth apt to be found with a fag in his mouth or stood on a table singing "Land of Hope and Glory" '?

14 **FOUR** Which batsman, who played for Cambridge University between 1950 and 1952, has scored the most centuries for the side?

15 **THREE** Christopher Cowdrey was selected for the 1984–85 tour of India and followed in his father's footsteps into the England team. But which off-spinner is the only cricketer to have played alongside both Sir Colin and Christopher Cowdrey in Test matches?

16 **SIX** Which current Lancashire batsman has hit 1058 runs in just 24 innings at Youth Test level?

17 **FOUR** Who did Ian Chappell replace as Australian skipper during the 1970–71 Ashes series?

18 **THREE** Who did South Africa beat at Port Elizabeth in December 1992 to register their first Test win in over 22 years?

19 **FOUR** Which Surrey and West Indies bowler disgraced himself when, furious at being pelted with fruit while fielding on the boundary in the final Test at Muyltan, Pakistan in 1980–81, he picked up a brick being used as a boundary marker and hurled it at a spectator, seriously injuring him?

20 **SIX** Which England swing bowler is the only man to take wickets with the first ball of two Test matches – Gavaskar at Edgbaston in 1974 and Morrison at Christchurch in 1974–75?

21 **FOUR** Which legendary England batsman narrowly missed becoming the first to score his 100th first-class hundred in a Test match when he hit 98 versus South Africa at Manchester in 1951?

22 **THREE** Which batsman, who was capped by England in 1991, hit 645 County Championship runs in 1990 without being dismissed?

23 **TWO** Which Gloucestershire bowler was left out of the 1992 West Indies World Cup squad despite taking 36 wickets for Jamaica in the Red Stripe Cup?

24 **FOUR** The Duchess of Norfolk XI beat the West Indies in their first match of the 1991 tour of England. Which Indian captain led the side?

25 **THREE** Which recent Yorkshire captain has played professional soccer with Bradford City?

SINGLES (6) Which six wicket-keepers made over 500 dismissals in first-class cricket in England in the 1980s?

INNINGS SCORE:

TEST CRICKET MISCELLANY

1   **TWO**   On which English Test ground would you find the Nursery End?

2   **FOUR**   Are Test cricketers Gladstone Small (England) and Milton Small (West Indies) related?

3   **TWO**   Who scored 1058 runs in 11 innings against New Zealand and India in 1990, becoming the first batsman to score over 1000 runs in Tests in an English summer?

4   **FOUR**   Which famous broadcaster's last Test match commentary was during the 1980 Centenary Test at Lord's?

5   **SIX**   (*Three runs each*) Which two bowlers took 34 and 32 wickets in the 1963 England-West Indies series?

6   **THREE**   Which England wicket-keeper hit 133 in only his 2nd Test against Australia at Perth in 1985?

7   **THREE**   Who scored 215 for Pakistan versus India at Lahore in 1982–83 to become the 20th batsman to score 100 first-class hundreds and only the second, after Boycott, to reach the milestone in a Test match?

8   **FOUR**   Who did Sri Lanka beat by nine wickets at Colombo in December 1992, registering their third Test match win?

9   **TWO**   Who hit a magnificent 174 in the 1977 Centenary Test?

10   **FOUR**   When Graham Gooch reached his memorable 300 against India in the Lord's Test of 1990, which batsman was at the other end?

11   **SIX**   Trevor Bailey was dismissed for a pair in his 61st and last Test. Which Australian bowler dismissed him in both innings?

12   **THREE**   Which New Zealand captain hit 176 at Trent Bridge in 1973 when the tourists amassed the highest 4th-innings score by a losing side in a Test match?

13   **FOUR**   Which spinner made his Australian Test debut in 1984–85, aged 38, after he had led New South Wales to a surprise win over the touring West Indians?

14   **TWO**   Who was the first West Indian wicket-keeper to claim 100 Test match dismissals?

15 **THREE** Which young Indian all-rounder, aged 19, was flown to New Zealand on the eve of the Wellington Test in 1980–81 and took 6–63 including three wickets in four balls?

16 **FOUR** Who in January 1992 became the first Western Samoan to play in Test cricket when he made his debut for New Zealand against England?

17 **THREE** Which Pakistan bowler took 12–165 in the 3rd Test at Sydney in 1976–77 to help his side to their first win on Australian soil?

18 **TWO** Which Australian wicket-keeper took 28 catches in the 1982–83 Ashes series?

19 **THREE** Which Englishman made his first Test hundred in his 54th innings during the 1st Test at Bombay in 1984–85?

20 **TWO** Who in his first Test series took 8–31 for England when India were bowled out for 58 at Leeds in 1952?

21 **SIX** Which South African-born Test batsman was Kapil Dev's 250th Test match victim at Bombay in 1984–85?

22 **SIX** Name the Sussex all-rounder who held five catches off Jim Laker's bowling in the famous 1956 Old Trafford Test.

23 **THREE** Which England batsman scored 1739 runs in Test cricket in 1974, including a memorable 262 not out at Sabina Park?

24 **FOUR** Which pair of brothers represented England against the West Indies at Trent Bridge in 1957, the first set of brothers to play alongside each other for England since the Hearnes (1891–92)?

25 **FOUR** Which seldom-used bowler took 6–32 for Pakistan at Lord's in 1982?

SINGLES (11) In May 1981, Middlesex became the first county side to name 11 Test match cricketers. Name that side.

INNINGS SCORE:

61

YORKSHIRE

1 **THREE** Who in 1973 took an 'A' Level examination at 6am so that he could make his first team debut for the county that day?

2 **FOUR** Which left-hander batted for 14 overs with a broken hand to deny Lancashire a Roses victory at Old Trafford in 1990?

3 **SIX** Who scored 203 against Yorkshire in a County Championship game in September 1988 to register the highest ever score by a Yorkshireman against Yorkshire?

4 **FOUR** Which batsman topped 1000 runs in 1987 to become the second youngest Yorkshireman, after Sir Leonard Hutton, to reach that milestone in a season?

5 **THREE** Who scored 146 versus Surrey in the 1965 Gillette Cup final?

6 **FOUR** Which bowler, now an established coach, took two hat-tricks in the 1966 season, versus Nottinghamshire (Worksop) and Kent (Harrogate)?

7 **TWO** Which famous cricketer was elected Young Cricketer of the Year in 1952?

8 **FOUR** Name the former Rhodesian policeman who took 113 wickets for Yorkshire in 1966.

9 **FOUR** Who, at Leeds in 1932, took 10–10 for Yorkshire against Nottinghamshire?

10 **SIX** Which batsman, who left the county at the end of 1991, scored 189 in the Roses Match at Scarborough earlier that season?

11 **FOUR** Which bowler, who made his Test debut in WG Grace's last England match, took 3608 wickets for the county between 1898 and 1930?

12 **THREE** Yorkshire won the County Championship for the last time in 1968. Who captained them that season?

13 **SIX** Which batsman, more recently seen as an umpire, was Man of the Match in the 1969 Gillette Cup final?

14 **FOUR** Which Yorkshire bowler, later to be capped by England, was suspended from bowling in 1972 by the TCCB owing to an unsatisfactory bowling action?

15 **SIX** Can you name the Yorkshire bowler and Middlesbrough centre-half who had to retire through injury?

16 **FOUR** Which Yorkshire bowler was flown out to join the 1979–80 tour of Australia and India as a replacement for the injured Mike Hendrick?

17 **FOUR** Who in 1990 became the first cricketer since Fred Trueman to make his Yorkshire first team debut without having played for the 2nd XI?

18 **FOUR** Who in 1983 scored 123 versus Nottinghamshire at Bradford on his first-class debut?

19 **THREE** Which wicket-keeper made 107 dismissals in the 1957 season?

20 **FOUR** Who in 1981 hit 116 on his first-class debut against Essex?

21 **THREE** Who, also in 1981, became the youngest wicket-keeper to play for Yorkshire?

22 **THREE** Name the Yorkshire cricketer who was named Young Cricketer of the Year in 1987.

23 **FOUR** Who captained Yorkshire from 1987 to 1989?

24 **SIX** Who in 1966 hit 30 off a Robin Hobbs over in the Yorkshire versus MCC game at Scarborough?

25 **FOUR** Which bowler, who had failed to score in 12 successive first-class innings in 1990, joined Yorkshire in 1991 from Northamptonshire?

SINGLES (7) When Yorkshire won the 1966 County Championship they played at which seven venues?

INNINGS SCORE:

62

TRIVIA

1 **FOUR** Which famous England fast bowler had the nickname of 'Trol'?

2 **SIX** What happened when the South Australian selectors picked an untried all-rounder as their 12th man in February 1976?

3 **THREE** Which England cricketer was once offered the throne of Albania?

4 **FOUR** What is the relationship between Bill and John Edrich?

5 **FOUR** Which famous Yorkshire bowler died in July 1943 from wounds sustained in Sicily whilst serving as a Captain in the Green Howards?

6 **FOUR** During the 1992 season, which Worcestershire player failed a routine drug test?

7 **THREE** Which England batsman was offered a trial with the New York Mets baseball team in 1990?

8 **SIX** Why was the rest day brought forward in the 1980 Golden Jubilee Test in Bombay?

9 **SIX** Which umpire was officiating when both David Lloyd and his son Graham scored their maiden first-class centuries?

10 **SIX** Why was Gloucestershire batsman Mark Alleyne arrested at Nairobi airport in November 1990?

11 **FOUR** What was unusual about the world record fifth-wicket stand of 464 set by two New South Wales batsmen versus Western Australia at Perth in 1990?

12 **THREE** What happened to Allan Lamb after he had scored 143 at Ballarat on the 1990–91 Ashes tour?

13 **FOUR** What do J J Ferris, Gil Mohammed, Kepler Wessels, W E Midwinter and Amir Elahi have in common?

14 **FOUR** What do the googly and television's *News at Ten* have in common?

15 **SIX** Why were there two tosses before the 3rd Test at Old Trafford during the 1989 Ashes series?

16   **FOUR**   When England were set 696 to win in the 'timeless Test' at Durban in 1938–39, they stood at 654–5 on the tenth day. Why did the match finish at that point?

17   **FOUR**   Which England cricketer was warned by police for making gestures to the crowd in the second one-day international versus India at Trent Bridge in 1990?

18   **FOUR**   Graham Gooch scored a triple century at Lord's versus India in 1990. Why did BBC Television not show him reaching this landmark?

19   **SIX**   What caused the postponement of the final England 'A' versus Kenya one-day game in 1990?

20   **FOUR**   Which England all-rounder was warned for intimidatory bowling in the 5th Test on the 1990 tour of the West Indies?

21   **SIX**   What was unusual about the selection of Navjot Singh Sidhu for India's tour of the West Indies in 1989?

22   **THREE**   Which former England captain has the christian names Edward Ralph?

23   **SIX**   CB Fry played in 26 Tests for England, but with which team did he win a FA Cup winners medal?

24   **THREE**   Who were the only brothers to play cricket for England in the 1980s?

25   **FOUR**   Against which commentator did umpire Lloyd Barker issue a writ after criticism of his performance in the 4th West Indies-England Test in 1990?

SINGLES (14) Name the 14 Minor County sides that will take part in the 1993 Nat West Trophy.

INNINGS SCORE:

ANSWERS

1. ONE DAY INTERNATIONALS

1. Canada **2.** Kapil Dev **3.** Papua New Guinea **4.** Graeme Hick **5.** John Bracewell **6.** Viv Richards **7.** Hit Wicket **8.** Andy Roberts **9.** Gary Gilmour **10.** Collis King **11.** Martin Sneddon **12.** Joel Garner **13.** Zimbabwe **14.** Dennis Amiss **15.** John Edrich **16.** Allan Lamb **17.** Michael Holding **18.** David Boon **19.** Graham Gooch **20.** Simon O'Donnell **21.** Dickie Bird **22.** Chetan Sharma **23.** Don Topley **24.** Neil Fairbrother **25.** Craig McDermott

Singles: Gooch, Robinson, Athey, Gatting, Lamb, Downton, Emburey, DeFreitas, Foster, Small and Hemmings.

2. BATTING I

1. Sir Jack Hobbs **2.** David Gower **3.** Alan Butcher **4.** Zaheer Abbas **5.** Mark Robinson **6.** Victoria **7.** Ken Barrington **8.** Sir Len Hutton **9.** Ian Botham **10.** Graeme Hick **11.** Dean Jones **12.** Bob Willis **13.** Sir Colin Cowdrey **14.** Chris Broad **15.** Jimmy Cook **16.** Brendan Kuruppu **17.** Matthew Maynard **18.** Graham Gooch **19.** Swansea **20.** Wally Hammond **21.** Everton Weekes **22.** Mike Gatting **23.** Geoff Boycott **24.** Mike Brearley **25.** Ian Redpath

Singles: Run Out, Timed Out, Handled Ball, Stumped, Caught, Hit Wicket, Hit Ball Twice, Bowled, LBW and Obstructing the Field.

3. DERBYSHIRE

1. Kim Barnett **2.** Fred Trueman **3.** Yorkshire **4.** Michael Holding **5.** Mohammed Azharuddin **6.** Peter Bowler **7.** Brian Bolus **8.** Michael Hendrick **9.** Chris Marples **10.** Geoff Miller **11.** Ian Buxton **12.** Dominic Cork **13.** Alan Ward **14.** Michael Hendrick **15.** Alan Ward **16.** Denmark **17.** Barry Wood **18.** Dallas Moir **19.** John Hampshire **20.** Bob Taylor **21.** Peter Kirsten **22.** Kim Barnett **23.** Devon Malcolm **24.** Geoff Miller **25.** John Morris.

Singles: Wright, Hill, Kirsten, Wood, Barnett, Steele, Miller, Tunnicliffe, Taylor, Newman and Hendrick.

4. ODDITIES

1. Larry Gomes **2.** Rob Andrew **3.** Graeme Wood **4.** Ian Botham **5.** Sewards **6.** Nigel Plews **7.** Michael Atherton **8.** Jim Higgs **9.** Hit Wicket **10.** John Major **11.** Len Pascoe **12.** Richard Ellison **13.** Lawrence Rowe **14.** Rev. David Sheppard **15.** Mrs Gandhi, the Indian Prime Minister, was assassinated **16.** Dickie Bird **17.** They refused to play on a Sunday. **18.** Bobby Simpson **19.** Mohsin Khan **20.** Viv Richards **21.** Ashley Mallett **22.** Majid Khan **23.** Simon Brown **24.** He tried to take pictures of the injured David Lawrence being stretchered off in agony. **25.** Bruce French.

Singles: Butcher, Cowans, DeFreitas, Lewis, Malcolm, Slack, Small and Williams.

5. AUSTRALIA

1. Handled the Ball 2. Eric Hollies 3. Neil Harvey 4. Mark Taylor 5. Queensland
6. Trevor Johns 7. Dean Jones 8. Merv Hughes 9. Peter Taylor 10. Worcestershire
11. Sir Don Bradman 12. Dean Jones 13. Rodney Marsh 14. Doug Walters 15.
Keith Miller 16. Alan Davidson 17. Geoff Lawson 18. Colin Milburn 19. David
Hookes or Wayne Phillips 20. Mike Veletta 21. Bruce Reid 22. Greg Matthews
23. Dean Jones 24. Doug Walters 25. Dean Jones
Singles: Lawry, Stackpole, I Chappell, G Chappell, Walters, Redpath, Sheehan,
Marsh, Jenner, O'Keeffe, McKenzie, Gleeson, A Thomson, Mallett, Connolly,
Duncan, Lillee, Eastwood and Dell.

6. COUNTY CHAMPIONSHIP

1. Gloucestershire (883) 2. Yorkshire (1202) 3. Surrey 4. Lancashire 5. Wilfred
Rhodes 6. Gloucestershire 7. Mike Procter 8. Yorkshire 9. Glamorgan 10. Bob
Willis 11. Essex 12. Fred Trueman, Tony Nicholson and Don Wilson 13.
Schweppes 14. Derbyshire 15. Somerset 16. Sir Jack Hobbs 17. 1977 18. Kent
19. AP 'Tich' Freeman 20. Warwickshire 21. Jimmy Cook 22. Worcestershire 23.
Sussex 24. Sir Richard Hadlee 25. Bob Willis.
Singles: Gloucestershire, Kent, Lancashire, Middlesex, Nottinghamshire, Surrey,
Sussex and Yorkshire.

7. DURHAM

1. Lance Cairns 2. Durham University 3. Yorkshire 4. John Glendenen 5. Chris
Scott 6. Dean Jones 7. Derbyshire 8. Geoff Cook 9. Staffordshire 10. Lancashire
11. Ian Botham 12. Phil Bainbridge 13. Paul Parker 14. John Glendenen 15.
Simon Davis 16. David Graveney 17. Ian Botham 18. Middlesex 19. Steve
McEwan 20. Paul Henderson 21. Wayne Larkins 22. Tony Wood 23. Glamorgan
24. Dean Jones 25. Yorkshire
Singles: Larkins, Glendenen, Jones, Parker, Bainbridge, Botham, Berry, Scott,
Graveney, Hughes and Brown.

8. MODERN CRICKETING HEROES I

GRAHAM GOOCH 1. Geoff Boycott 2. Bobby Simpson 3. Greg Chappell 4. Sir
Don Bradman 5. Geoff Boycott 6. West Indies
SIR RICHARD HADLEE 7. Asif Iqbal 8. Tasmania 9. Dayle 10. Devon Malcolm
11. Lord's 12. Lancaster Park, Christchurch
IAN BOTHAM 13. Greg Chappell, 14. Sunil Gavaskar 15. Vinoo Mankad 16.
Alan Knott 17. Lancaster Park, Christchurch 18. Rodney Marsh and Jeffrey Dujon
VIV RICHARDS 19. The Oval 20. Brian Close 21. Surrey 22. Queensland 23.
Warwickshire 24. Old Trafford 25. Ian Botham
Singles: Boycott, Barrington, Botham and Hammond.

ANSWERS

9. WORLD CUP 1992

1. Pakistan **2.** Graham Gooch **3.** David Shepherd **4.** Phil Tufnell **5.** Dennis Amiss
6. Neil Fairbrother **7.** They have all batted first **8.** Eddo Brandes **9.** Inzamam-ul-
Haq **10.** Wasim Akram **11.** John Traicos **12.** Viv Richards **13.** Dermot Reeve **14.**
Graham Gooch, Phil DeFreitas and Allan Lamb **15.** Martin Crowe **16.** Ramiz Raja
17. South Africa **18.** Ian Botham **19.** Sri Lanka **20.** Craig McDermott **21.** Anderson
Cummins **22.** West Indies **23.** Imran Khan **24.** Martin Crowe **25.** New Zealand
Singles: Aamir Sohail, Ramiz Raja, Imran Khan, Javed Miandad, Inzamam-ul-Haq,
Wasim Akram, Salim Malik, Ijaz Ahmed, Moin Khan, Mushtaq Ahmed and Aqib
Javed.

10. ESSEX

1. Graham Gooch **2.** Westcliff **3.** David Acfield **4.** Graham Saville **5.** David East
6. Mark Ilott **7.** Keith Boyce **8.** Brian Taylor **9.** Trevor Bailey **10.** Robin Hobbs **11.**
Keith Fletcher **12.** Barrie Knight **13.** Doug Insole **14.** Ken McEwan **15.** Neil Foster
16. Brian Hardie **17.** Salim Malik **18.** Kenya **19.** Stuart Turner **20.** John Lever **21.**
France **22.** Trevor Bailey **23.** Keith Boyce **24.** Victoria **25.** Southend
Singles: Denness, Gooch, McEwan, Fletcher, Hardie, K Pont, Phillip, Turner, Smith,
R East and Lever.

11. SPINNERS

1. Eddie Hemmings **2.** Fred Titmus **3.** Bishen Bedi **4.** John Bracewell **5.** Fred
Trueman **6.** Pat Pocock **7.** Robin Hobbs **8.** Ian Folley **9.** Derek Underwood **10.** He
handled the ball **11.** John Emburey **12.** Nick Cook **13.** Eddie Hemmings **14.**
Derek Underwood **15.** Jim Laker **16.** Lance Gibbs **17.** Abdul Qadir **18.** Bob
Holland **19.** Fred Titmus **20.** Peter Petherick **21.** Sonny Ramadhin **22.** Richie
Benaud **23.** Hampshire **24.** Harvey Trump **25.** Phil Edmonds
Singles: Gibbs, Underwood, Bedi, Benaud, Chandrasekhar, Abdul Qadir and
Grimmett.

12. ASHES TESTS I

1. Wilfred Rhodes **2.** Derek Randall **3.** Bob Massie **4.** John Dyson **5.** The Oval **6.**
Steve Barwick **7.** Mike Denness **8.** Jeff Thomson **9.** Rodney Marsh **10.** Geoff Miller
11. Melbourne **12.** Warwick Armstrong **13.** Bob Wyatt **14.** Dennis Compton **15.**
Bill Ponsford **16.** Angus Fraser **17.** George Davis **18.** John Edrich **19.** Sir Colin
Cowdrey **20.** Dennis Lillee **21.** Chris Old **22.** John Snow **23.** Richard Ellison **24.**
Kim Hughes **25.** Geoff Lawson
Singles: Richardson, Cowdrey, Rev. Shepperd, May, Bailey, Washbrook, Oakman,
Evans, Lock and Statham.

13. INDIA
1. Ted Dexter 2. Sandeep Patil 3. Sunil Gavaskar 4. Mohinder Armanath 5. Kapil Dev 6. Somerset 7. Five batsmen had retired hurt 8. Kapil Dev 9. Lord's 10. Manoj Prabhakar 11. Bhagwat Chandrasekhar 12. Ravi Shastri 13. Dilip Vengsarkar 14. Vijay Manjrekar 15. Port of Spain 16. Lord's 17. Yadurvindra Singh 18. Bombay 19. Mohinder Armanath 20. Nahinder Hirwani 21. Mohammed Azharuddin 22. Gundappa Viswanath 23. Bishen Bedi 24. SP 'Fergie' Gupte 25. Derbyshire

Singles: Gavaskar, Srikkanth, Armanath, Azharuddin, Shastri, Pandit, Kapil Dev, More, Sharma, Yadav and Maninder Singh.

14. GLAMORGAN
1. Huw Morris 2. Ezra Moseley 3. Viv Richards 4. Majid Khan 5. Tony Cordle 6. Tony Lewis 7. John Hopkins 8. Sussex 9. Alan Jones 10. Alan Rees 11. Peter Walker 12. Don Shepherd 13. Neath 14. Malcolm Nash 15. Roy Fredericks 16. Huw Morris 17. Middlesex 18. Matthew Maynard 19. Alan Jones 20. Hamish Anthony 21. Matthew Maynard 22. Malcolm Nash 23. Jimmy Cook 24. Robin Hobbs 25. Cardiff

Singles: Clay, A Jones, J Jones, Lewis, McConnon, Maynard, H Morris, Parkhouse, Thomas, Walker, Watkin and Watkins.

15. DOMESTIC ONE-DAY CRICKET
1. Norman Gifford 2. Ken McEwan 3. John Mortimore 4. They beat them in a 'bowl-off' 5. Geoff Boycott 6. Brian Hardie 7. Hampshire 8. Northamptonshire 9. Cheshire 10. David Hughes 11. Ireland 12. Jeff Thomson 13. Graham McKenzie 14. Somerset (1981–2) 15. Graham Rose 16. Lancashire 17. Graham Lloyd 18. David Bairstow 19. Brian Rose 20. Durham 21. Jack Simmons 22. Alan Fordham 23. Wayne Daniel 24. Brian Langford 25. Raymond Illingworth

Singles: Geoff Boycott (1965 Gillette), Clive Lloyd (1972 Gillette), Graham Gooch (1979 B & H), Viv Richards (1979 Gillette and 1981 B & H), Geoff Cook (1981 Nat West) and Brian Hardie (1985 Nat West).

16. BOWLERS I
1. Clarrie Grimmett 2. Derek Underwood 3. Pat Pocock 4. Courtney Walsh 5. Dennis Lillee 6. John Emburey 7. Dilip Vengsarkar 8. Richard Illingworth 9. Sonny Ramadhin 10. Ireland 11. Tony Greig 12. John Snow 13. Tony Lock 14. Tom Cartwright 15. Allan Border 16. Jack Birkenshaw 17. Essex 18. Bob Willis 19. Ian Botham 20. Greg Matthews 21. Chris Pringle 22. Abdul Qadir 23. Bill Voce 24. Chris Lewis 25. Phil Simmons

Singles: Atherton, Barnett, Botham, Capel, Cook, Curtis, DeFreitas, Dilley, Emburey, Foster, Fraser, Gooch, Hemmings, Igglesden, Jarvis, Malcolm, Newport, Pringle and Small.

17. GLOUCESTERSHIRE

1. WG Grace **2.** David Lawrence **3.** Tony Brown **4.** Gloucester **5.** David Allen **6.** Mike Procter **7.** Arthur Milton **8.** Somerset **9.** Courtney Walsh **10.** Tony Wright **11.** Kevin Curran **12.** Alistair Hignell **13.** Wally Hammond **14.** John Mortimore **15.** Sadiq Mohammed **16.** David Shepherd **17.** Mike Procter **18.** Chris Broad **19.** John Shepherd **20.** Jack Russell **21.** Yorkshire **22.** John Childs **23.** Bristol **24.** Australia **25.** Robert

Singles: Sadiq Mohammed, Knight, Zaheer Abbas, Procter, D Shepherd, Stovold, Brown, Foat, Graveney, Mortimore and Davey.

18. DEBUTS

1. Sir Len Hutton **2.** John Hampshire **3.** Hobart, Tasmania **4.** Martin Jean-Jacques **5.** Alec Bedser **6.** Neil Fairbrother **7.** None **8.** Chris Balderstone **9.** Ian Botham **10.** Peter Bowler **11.** Damien Martyn **12.** Monte Lynch **13.** Mark Ramprakash **14.** Vincent Van Der Bijl **15.** Omar Henry **16.** Clayton Lambert **17.** 1983 (for Zimbabwe) **18.** Graham Dilley **19.** Martyn Moxon **20.** Wasim Akram **21.** Keith Fletcher **22.** John Childs **23.** Doug Walters **24.** Mark Greatbatch **25.** Trevor Jesty

Singles: Parker (Durham), Stephenson (Essex), Maynard (Glamorgan), Benson, Igglesden (both Kent), Whitaker (Leicestershire), Williams (Middlesex), Pigott (Sussex) and Lloyd (Warwickshire).

19. COMEBACKS

1. Godfrey Evans **2.** Brian Close **3.** Jon Agnew **4.** Pat Pocock **5.** Younis Ahmed **6.** Ken Higgs **7.** Phil Edmonds **8.** Bobby Simpson **9.** David Bairstow **10.** Worcestershire **11.** Bob Taylor **12.** Tom Graveney **13.** Ashley Mallett **14.** Sir Colin Cowdrey **15.** John Lever **16.** Brian Luckhurst **17.** Bradford **18.** Peter Willey **19.** Jim Parks **20.** Tony Lock **21.** Mike Smith **22.** Wayne Larkins **23.** David Steele **24.** Richie Benaud **25.** Raymond Illingworth

Singles: Gooch, Boycott, Brearley, Gower, Gatting, Willey, Botham, Taylor, Dilley, Old, and Willis.

20. HAMPSHIRE

1. Bob Cottam **2.** Bobby Parks **3.** Derek Shackleton **4.** Paul Terry **5.** Colin Mead **6.** Gordon Greenidge **7.** Chris Smith **8.** Roy Marshall **9.** Stephen Jeffries **10.** Barry Richards **11.** Andy Roberts **12.** Robin Smith **13.** Gordon Greenidge **14.** Peter Sainsbury **15.** Bob Stephenson **16.** Colin Ingleby-Mackenzie **17.** Malcolm Marshall **18.** Richard Gilliat **19.** Derek Shackleton **20.** David Gower **21.** Headingley **22.** Aqib Javed **23.** Mark Nicholas **24.** Jean-Paul Bakker **25.** Malcolm Marshall

Singles: Gilliat, Greenidge, Herman, Jesty, Lewis, Mottram, Murtagh, O'Sullivan, Richards, Sainsbury, Stephenson, Taylor and Turner.

21. ENGLISH TEST CRICKET I

1. Neil Williams **2.** David Gower **3.** Ken Barrington **4.** Gladstone Small **5.** Shakoor Rana **6.** Chris Tavare **7.** Sir Jack Hobbs **8.** Brian Statham **9.** Peter Loader **10.** Johnny Wardle **11.** Wally Hammond **12.** Mike Gatting **13.** Clive Radley **14.** Peter Lever **15.** John Lever **16.** Chris Old **17.** Geoff Cook **18.** Fifteen **19.** India **20.** Ian Botham **21.** Geoff Boycott **22.** John Edrich **23.** Bramall Lane, Sheffield **24.** Wilfred Rhodes **25.** Gubby Allen
Singles: Gooch, Bailey, Barnett, Childs, Dilley, Emburey, Foster, Gower, Hemmings, Lamb, Lawrence, Newport, Robinson, Rhodes, Russell and R Smith.

22. NEW ZEALAND

1. Glenn Turner **2.** Ewan Chatfield **3.** Lance Cairns **4.** Adam Parore **5.** Geoff Howarth **6.** Colin Croft **7.** Napier **8.** Wellington **9.** Mark Burgess **10.** Glenn Turner **11.** John Reid **12.** John Parker **13.** Ken Rutherford **14.** Bev Congdon, Geoff Howarth and Glenn Turner **15.** Central Districts **16.** West Indies **17.** Shell Trophy **18.** Lancashire **19.** Christchurch **20.** Glenn Turner **21.** John Wright **22.** Sri Lanka **23.** Ewan Chatfield **24.** Richard Collinge **25.** Somerset
Singles: Lowry, Page, W Hadlee, Rabone, Reid, Sinclair, Chapple, Dowling, Congdon, Burgess, Howarth, Coney, J Crowe and Wright.

23. ALL ROUNDERS I

1. Mike Watkinson **2.** Mike Procter **3.** John Emburey, Phil Carrick and Mike Watkinson **4.** Wasim Akram **5.** Mike Procter **6.** Brian Close **7.** Sussex **8.** Rachael Heyhoe-Flint **9.** Derek Pringle **10.** Kent **11.** Trevor Bailey **12.** Wilfred Wooller **13.** Kapil Dev **14.** Ian Botham **15.** Bruce Taylor **16.** Collie Smith **17.** Kapil Dev **18.** Franklyn Stephenson **19.** Kapil Dev **20.** David Capel **21.** Ian Pont **22.** Wasim Akram **23.** Dermot Reeve **24.** Derbyshire **25.** Steve Waugh
Singles: Cairns, Croft, Curran, Emburey and Lewis.

24. KENT

1. Derek Underwood **2.** Bob Woolmer **3.** Alan Ealham **4.** Tunbridge Wells **5.** Arthur Fagg **6.** Carl Hooper **7.** Mike Denness **8.** Maidstone **9.** Alan Knott **10.** Asif Iqbal **11.** Canterbury **12.** Graham Dilley **13.** Sir Colin Cowdrey **14.** John Graham **15.** David Nicholls **16.** Middlesex **17.** Graham Johnson **18.** Derek Underwood **19.** Neil Taylor **20.** John Shepherd **21.** Frank Woolley **22.** Folkestone **23.** Asif Iqbal **24.** Neil Taylor **25.** Brian Luckhurst
Singles: Benson, Sir Colin Cowdrey, Christopher Cowdrey, Denness, Dilley, Ellison, Igglesden, Knott, Luckhurst, Tavare, Underwood and Woolmer.

25. MODERN CRICKETING HEROES II
ALLAN BORDER 1. Essex and Gloucestershire **2.** David Boon **3.** Graham Yallop
4. Queensland and New South Wales **5.** Mike Brearley **6.** Kim Hughes
DAVID GOWER 7. Raymond Illingworth **8.** Edgbaston **9.** Bob Willis **10.** Ivon **11.**
Pakistan **12.** India
DENNIS LILLEE 13. Northamptonshire **14.** Rest of the World XI **15.** Javed
Miandad **16.** Mike Brearley **17.** 1981 **18.** Lance Gibbs
CLIVE LLOYD 19. Frank Hayes **20.** Geoff Arnold **21.** Warwickshire **22.** Guyana
23. Rohan Kanhai **24.** Dermot Reeve **25.** 1968
Singles: Baptiste, Davis, Dujon, Garner, Gomes, Greenidge, Harper, Haynes,
Holding, Marshall, Richards, Richardson, Small and Walsh.

26. LEFT-HANDERS
1. John Dye **2.** Brian Close **3.** Huw Morris **4.** Richard Illingworth **5.** John Edrich **6.**
Graeme Fowler **7.** Alan Davidson **8.** Darren Bicknell **9.** Bruce Reid **10.** Graham
Yallop **11.** Mark Taylor **12.** David Gower **13.** Kevin Sharp **14.** Graham Thorpe
15. Geoff Dymock **16.** David Lloyd **17.** Phil Tufnell **18.** Neil Fairbrother **19.** Brian
Rose **20.** Neil Harvey **21.** Graeme Fowler **22.** Fred Rumsey **23.** Neil Harvey **24.**
Chris Broad **25.** John Lever
Singles: Benson, Broad, Childs, Dilley, Ellison, Fairbrother, Fowler, Gower, A
Lloyd, Old, Rose, Russell, Slack and D Smith.

27. LANCASHIRE
1. Harry Pilling **2.** Matthew Hilton **3.** Barry Wood **4.** Frank Hayes **5.** Jack Simmons
6. Ken Higgs **7.** Sussex **8.** Andrew Kennedy **9.** Clive Lloyd **10.** Frank Hayes **11.**
David Lloyd **12.** Brian Statham **13.** Ian Austin **14.** Steve O'Shaughnessy **15.** Colin
Croft **16.** David Hughes **17.** Gary Yates **18.** Archie MacLaren **19.** Neil Fairbrother
20. Peter Lee **21.** Mike Watkinson **22.** Soren Henriksen **23.** Michael Holding **24.**
David Green **25.** Graeme Fowler
Singles: D Lloyd, Wood, Pilling, C Lloyd, Sullivan, Engineer, Bond, Hughes,
Simmons, Shuttleworth and Lever.

28. ENGLAND V PAKISTAN
1. Robin Smith **2.** Zaheer Abbas **3.** Hanif, Sadiq and Mushtaq **4.** Richard Blakey **5.**
Intikhab Alam **6.** Salim Malik **7.** Ted Dexter **8.** Asif Mujtaba **9.** Imran Khan **10.**
Javed Miandad **11.** Roy Palmer **12.** Aamir Sohail **13.** West Indies (v Sri Lanka,
Karachi 1987) **14.** The Oval **15.** Wasim Bari **16.** Javed Miandad **17.** Dennis
Compton **18.** Alan Knott **19.** Atar Rehman **20.** Alec Stewart **21.** Mudassar Nazar
22. Nick Cook **23.** Graeme Hick **24.** Neil Mallender **25.** Graham Gooch
Singles: Gooch, Broad, Athey, Robinson, N Cook, Capel, Emburey, Foster, French
and Hemmings.

29. CAPTAINS

1. Graham Gooch 2. Sir Colin Cowdrey 3. Sir Len Hutton 4. Richie Benaud 5. Mike Gatting 6. David Graveney 7. Mickey Stewart 8. Christopher Cowdrey 9. Clive Rice 10. Bobby Simpson 11. Tony Lewis 12. Somerset 13. Ted Dexter 14. Kim Hughes 15. Bobby Simpson 16. Mike Brearley 17. Allan Lamb 18. Alvin Kallicharran 19. Richie Benaud 20. Jimmy Cook 21. Peter May 22. Graham Gooch 23. Kim Hughes 24. Bishen Bedi 25. Keith Fletcher

Singles: Hammond, Yardley, Brown, Hutton, May, Colin Cowdrey, Dexter, MJK Smith, Graveney, Illingworth, Denness, J Edrich, Greig, Brearley, Botham, Willis, Gower, Gatting, Gooch and Lamb.

30. ENGLAND V WEST INDIES

1. Michael Holding 2. Frank Hayes 3. Graeme Hick 4. Allan Lamb 5. Geoff Boycott 6. Ian Allen 7. Gus Logie 8. Derek Pringle 9. Graham Gooch 10. Andy Roberts 11. Dennis Amiss 12. Huw Morris 13. David Smith 14. Peter Loader 15. Lawrence Rowe 16. Paul Terry 17. Phil Tufnell 18. Peter Willey 19. Sir Garfield Sobers and Michael Holding 20. George Headley 21. Viv Richards 22. Malcolm Marshall 23. Andy Lloyd 24. Ken Higgs 25. Winston Davis

Singles (11): Gooch, Larkins, Stewart, Lamb, Smith, Hussain, Capel, Russell, Small, Fraser and Malcolm.

31. LEICESTERSHIRE

1. Chris Balderstone 2. Ken Higgs 3. John Steele 4. Roger Tolchard 5. Barry Dudleston 6. Brian Davison 7. Minor Counties 8. David Gower 9. Tony Lock 10. Bobby Simpson 11. Graham Cross 12. Jack Birkenshaw 13. Ray Illingworth 14. Graham McKenzie 15. David Millns 16. Brian Davison 17. Clive Inman 18. Chris Lewis 19. Ken Higgs 20. Tim Boon 21. Winston Benjamin 22. James Whitaker 23. Ray Julien 24. Northamptonshire 25. Nigel Briers

Singles: Dudleston, Norman, Tolchard, Davison, Balderstone, Illingworth, Haywood, Steele, McKenzie, Higgs and Spencer.

32. WICKET-KEEPERS

1. Kieran More 2. John Murray 3. Warren Hegg 4. Ian Smith 5. Bruce French, Bill Athey, Bobby Parks and Bob Taylor 6. Leslie Ames 7. Mike Garnham 8. Bob Taylor 9. He stumped three consecutive Somerset batsmen off successive balls 10. Wasim Bari 11. Bob Taylor 12. Dennis Lindsay 13. Steve Marsh 14. Sri Lanka 15. Alan Knott 16. Geoff Humpage 17. Jimmy Binks 18. Jack Russell 19. Roger Tolchard 20. Deryck Murray 21. Brian Taylor 22. Ian Gould 23. Tim Zoehrer 24. Colin Boulton 25. Godfrey Evans

Singles: Bairstow, Downton, French, Knott, Richards, Russell and Taylor.

33. PAKISTAN

1. Mushtaq Mohammed **2.** Saeed Ahmed **3.** Fazal Mahmood **4.** Run Out **5.** Mudassar Nazar **6.** Intikhab Alam **7.** Sarfraz Nawaz **8.** Khalid Ibadulla **9.** Javed Miandad **10.** Hanif Mohammed **11.** Wasim Raja **12.** West Indies **13.** Imran Khan **14.** Auckland **15.** Mohsin Kamal **16.** Kent **17.** Majid Khan **18.** Intikhab Alam **19.** Salim Malik **20.** Taslim Arif **21.** Karachi **22.** Ramiz Raja **23.** Intikhab Alam **24.** Javed Miandad **25.** Wasim Bari

Singles: Javed Burki, Sadiq Mohammed, Saaed Ahmed, Asif Iqbal, Mushtaq Mohammed, Shafqat Rana, Intikhab Alam, Wasim Bari, Salim Altat, Sarfraz Nawaz and Pervez Sajjad.

34. BATTING II

1. Mickey Stewart, John Edrich, and Ken Barrington **2.** Glenn Turner **3.** Sachin Tendulkar **4.** Chris Tavare **5.** Graham Yallop **6.** Graham Gooch **7.** Trevor Jesty **8.** Javed Miandad **9.** John Morris **10.** Viv Richards **11.** Mike Atherton **12.** Paul Prichard **13.** Allan Lamb **14.** David Gower **15.** Glenn Turner **16.** Tim Robinson **17.** David Hookes **18.** Vic Pollard **19.** Sir Jack Hobbs **20.** Dennis Amiss **21.** Glenn Turner and Phil Neale **22.** Javed Miandad **23.** Somerset **24.** Tony Middleton **25.** Tim Curtis

Singles: Bradman (twice), Cowper, Hanif Mohammed, Rowe, Simpson and Sobers.

35. MIDDLESEX

1. Paul Farbrace **2.** Larry Gomes **3.** Denis Compton **4.** Mike Brearley **5.** Lancashire **6.** Fred Titmus **7.** Mike Gatting **8.** Surrey **9.** Mark Ramprakash **10.** Norman Cowans **11.** Graham Barlow **12.** John Murray **13.** Peter Parfitt **14.** Wayne Daniel **15.** Ricardo Ellcock **16.** John Emburey **17.** Brighton & Hove Albion **18.** Desmond Haynes **19.** Simon Hughes **20.** Zambia (formerly Northern Rhodesia) **21.** Dean Headley **22.** Surrey **23.** Fred Titmus **24.** John Price **25.** Yorkshire

Singles: Barlow, Brearley, Butcher, Cowans, Downton, Edmonds, Emburey, Fraser, Gatting, Parfitt, Price, Radley, Selvey, Slack and Titmus.

36. VENUES

1. Arundel **2.** Bristol **3.** Gloucestershire **4.** Trent Bridge **5.** Old Trafford **6.** Shropshire **7.** Hampshire **8.** Melbourne **9.** Great Britain **10.** Portsmouth **11.** Calcutta **12.** Melbourne **13.** Perth **14.** Prince's Ground **15.** Old Trafford **16.** Southend **17.** Skydome, Toronto **18.** Edgbaston **19.** Old Trafford **20.** Southend **21.** Bridgetown, Barbados **22.** Kent **23.** Taunton **24.** Middlesex **25.** Old Trafford

Singles: Darlington, Durham University, Gateshead Fell, Hartlepool, Jesmond and Stockton.

37. MILESTONES

1. David Gower **2.** Hanif Mohammed **3.** Graeme Pollock **4.** David Capel **5.** Trevor Bailey **6.** Sydney **7.** Kevin Shine **8.** Franklyn Stephenson **9.** Anton Ferreira **10.** Kingston, Jamaica **11.** Neil Hawke **12.** Aqib Javed **13.** Wayne Larkins **14.** Martin Sneddon **15.** Sanjay Manjrekar **16.** Lee Germon **17.** Sussex **18.** Derek Randall (in the Notts v Derbyshire game the original square was deemed unsuitable and a second pitch was used) **19.** Malcolm Marshall **20.** Rod Marsh **21.** Jack Birkenshaw **22.** Brisbane **23.** Ian Botham **24.** Nahinder Hirwani **25.** Sir Colin Cowdrey

Singles: Hobbs, Hendren, Hammond, Mead and Boycott.

38. NORTHAMPTONSHIRE

1. Wayne Larkins **2.** Dennis Brookes **3.** Kapil Dev **4.** Sarfraz Nawaz **5.** Mushtaq Mohammed **6.** David Steele **7.** Robin Bailey **8.** Leicestershire **9.** David Capel **10.** Greg Thomas **11.** Robin Bailey **12.** Lancashire **13.** Roger Prideaux **14.** Eldine Baptiste **15.** Bishen Bedi **16.** Allan Lamb **17.** Raman Subba Row **18.** Mushtaq Mohammed **19.** Neil Mallender **20.** Alan Fordham **21.** David Larter **22.** Roger Harper **23.** Peter Willey **24.** Somerset **25.** Kevin Curran

Singles: Cook, Larkins, A Lamb, Williams, Willey, Yardley, Sharp, Sarfraz Nawaz, Mallender, T Lamb and Griffiths.

39. ASHES TESTS II

1. Mark Waugh **2.** Ian Botham **3.** Terry Alderman **4.** Rodney Hogg **5.** Gladstone Small **6.** Tim Robinson **7.** Alec Bedser, Ian Botham, Derek Underwood and Bob Willis **8.** Allan Border **9.** Rick McCosker **10.** Kim Hughes **11.** Sir Don Bradman **12.** Craig McDermott **13.** Graham Dilley **14.** Geoff Boycott **15.** Phil Newport **16.** Derek Randall **17.** Keith Miller **18.** Carl Rackemann **19.** Bob Woolmer **20.** David Brown **21.** Norman Cowans **22.** Mike Denness **23.** Eddie Hemmings **24.** Allan Border **25.** Neil Harvey

Singles: Alderman, Boon, Campbell, Healy, Hohns, Hughes, Jones, Lawson, Marsh, M Taylor and S Waugh.

40. AROUND THE COUNTIES

1. Richard Davis and Minal Patel **2.** Jimmy Cook **3.** Middlesex **4.** Steve Marsh **5.** Derbyshire **6.** Tom Moody **7.** Northamptonshire **8.** Paul Jarvis **9.** Essex **10.** Matthew Fleming **11.** Paul Allott and Graeme Fowler **12.** Phil Neale **13.** Johnny Wardle **14.** Geoff Lawson **15.** Eddie Hemmings **16.** Franklyn Stephenson **17.** Peter Such **18.** Chelmsford, Essex **19.** Middlesbrough **20.** Derek Underwood **21.** Mike Garnham **22.** Somerset **23.** Northamptonshire **24.** Rodney Ontong **25.** Headingley

Singles: Derbyshire, Durham, Gloucestershire, Lancashire, Northamptonshire, Somerset and Sussex.

41. NOTTINGHAMSHIRE

1. Andy Afford **2.** Mark Crawley **3.** Middlesex **4.** Kenya **5.** Clive Rice **6.** Warwickshire **7.** Sir Richard Hadlee **8.** Derek Randall **9.** Bruce French **10.** Kevin Cooper **11.** Chris Broad **12.** Derek Randall **13.** Franklyn Stephenson **14.** Chris Broad **15.** Leicestershire **16.** Swansea **17.** Bruce French **18.** Sir Gary Sobers **19.** Clive Rice **20.** WG Grace **21.** Deryck Murray **22.** Paul Johnson **23.** Keith Miller **24.** Dusty Hare **25.** Sir Richard Hadlee

Singles: Birch, Bore, Cooper, Dexter, French, Hacker, Hadlee, Harris, Hassan, Hemmings, Randall, Rice, Robinson, Saxelby, Todd and Weightman.

42. ALL-ROUNDERS II

1. Geoff Miller **2.** Dipak Patel **3.** Chris Cairns **4.** Sir Garfield Sobers **5.** Graham Stevenson **6.** Keith Boyce **7.** Tony Greig **8.** Ian Botham **9.** Wasim Akram **10.** Keith Miller **11.** Arnie Sidebottom **12.** Jack Birkenshaw **13.** Collis King **14.** Greg Matthews **15.** Barrie Knight **16.** Martin Donnelly **17.** Chris Old **18.** Mike Procter **19.** Kevin Curran **20.** Dermot Reeve **21.** WG Grace **22.** Phil Carrick **23.** Mark Taylor **24.** Bernard Julien **25.** Norbert Philip

Singles: Allen, Bradman, Cowdrey, Hadlee, Hobbs, Hutton, Leveson-Gower, Sobers, Warner and Worrell.

43. MODERN CRICKETING HEROES III

IMRAN KHAN 1. Sussex **2.** Oxford University **3.** Ian Botham **4.** Intikhab Alam **5.** 1987 **6.** Majid Kham

SUNIL GAVASKAR 7. West Indies **8.** Bishen Bedi **9.** John Snow **10.** Geoffrey Boycott **11.** Kapil Dev **12.** The Oval

GREG CHAPPELL 13. His brother Trevor **14.** Sir Colin Cowdrey **15.** South Australia and Queensland **16.** Somerset **17.** They all scored hundreds in their first and last Test match appearances **18.** Sir Don Bradman

GEOFFREY BOYCOTT 19. Herbert Sutcliffe and Sir Len Hutton **20.** Keith Fletcher **21.** Michael Parkinson **22.** Brian Close **23.** South Africa **24.** He beat Sir Gary Sobers' Test run aggregate record **25.** Australia

Singles: Amiss, Barber, Barrington, Brearley, A Butcher, Sir C Cowdrey, Edrich, Gooch, Larkins, Luckhurst, Milburn, Murray, Randall, Rose, Russell and Titmus.

44. SOMERSET

1. Andy Hayhurst **2.** Northamptonshire **3.** Chris Tavare **4.** Holland **5.** Kenneth MacLeay **6.** Viv Richards **7.** Peter Roebuck **8.** Ian Botham **9.** Greg Chappell **10.** Sussex **11.** Brian Close **12.** Viv Marks **13.** Jimmy Cook **14.** Neil Mallender **15.** Roland Lefebvre **16.** Brian Langford **17.** Roy Virgin **18.** Ken Palmer **19.** Kerry O'Keeffe **20.** Brian Close **21.** Bill Alley **22.** Martin Crowe **23.** David Graveney **24.** Arthur Wellard **25.** Peter Denning

Singles: Rose, Denning, Richards, Roebuck, Botham, Marks, Burgess, Breakwell, Garner, Taylor and Jennings.

45. INTO THE NINETIES

1. Mushtaq Ahmed **2.** Middlesex **3.** Michael Atherton **4.** Huw Morris **5.** Chris Cowdrey **6.** Keith Fletcher **7.** Paul Taylor and Richard Blakey **8.** Dermot Reeve **9.** Equity and Law **10.** He was handed a writ **11.** Kim Barnett **12.** John Emburey **13.** Ian Salisbury **14.** John Crawley (Cambridge University) and Mark Crawley (Nottinghamshire) **15.** Richie Richardson **16.** Allan Border **17.** Michael Roseberry, Mike Gatting and Peter Bowler **18.** India **19.** Dickie Bird **20.** Graeme Fowler **21.** Greg Matthews **22.** Bob Willis **23.** John Hampshire **24.** Durham **25.** Dickie Bird
Singles: Archer, Broad, Cairns, Crawley, Dessaur, Evans, Johnson, Lewis, Randall, Robinson and Wileman.

46. SOUTH AFRICA

1. Barry Richards **2.** Peter Pollock **3.** Peter van der Meuwe **4.** Alan Wells **5.** Ali Bacher **6.** Kepler Wessels **7.** Graeme Pollock **8.** Denis Lindsay **9.** Andrew Hudson **10.** Barry Richards **11.** Sir Gary Sobers **12.** MJK Smith **13.** Jimmy Cook **14.** Currie Cup **15.** Eddie Barlow **16.** Mike Procter **17.** Hugh Tayfield **18.** Jackie McGlew **19.** Johannesburg **20.** Peter Kirsten **21.** Daryll Cullinan **22.** He handled the ball after a collision with a fielder **23.** Richie Benaud **24.** Vincent van der Bijl **25.** Allan Donald
Singles: Rushmere, Hudson, Wessels, Kirsten, Cronje, Kuiper, Richardson, Snell, Pringle, Donald and Bosch.

47. SURREY

1. John Edrich **2.** Mickey Stewart **3.** Stewart Storey **4.** Wales **5.** Arnold Long **6.** David Gower **7.** Geoff Arnold **8.** Graham Roope **9.** Mickey Stewart **10.** Pat Pocock **11.** Dudley Owen-Thomas **12.** Geoff Howarth **13.** Andrew Sandham **14.** Tony Lock **15.** Kent **16.** Essex **17.** Ian Greig **18.** Waqar Younis **19.** Percy Fender **20.** Sylvester Clarke **21.** Intikhab Alam **22.** India **23.** Younis Ahmed **24.** Bob Willis **25.** Sir Jack Hobbs
Singles: Arnold, Butcher, Edrich, Jackman, Pocock, Roope, Richards, A Stewart and Willis.

48. ENGLAND ON TOUR

1. David Gower **2.** Graham Gooch **3.** Ian Smith **4.** Ezra Moseley **5.** Chris Broad **6.** Tony Lock **7.** Fred Titmus **8.** Devon Malcolm **9.** Clive Radley **10.** Neil Mallender **11.** Dennis Lillee **12.** Derek Randall **13.** Ken Barrington **14.** Tom Cartwright **15.** Richard Illingworth **16.** Jack Russell **17.** Graham Gooch **18.** Brian Close **19.** Bill Athey **20.** Graham Gooch **21.** Mike Brearley **22.** Norman Gifford **23.** Wilf Slack **24.** Doug Insole **25.** Ian Botham
Singles: Woolmer, Brearley, Underwood, Randall, Amiss, Fletcher, Greig, Knott, Old, Lever and Willis.

49. BOWLERS II

1. Craig McDermott 2. David Lawrence 3. Robin Jackman 4. Graham Dilley 5. Martin McCague 6. Wasim Akram 7. Phil DeFreitas 8. Richard Snell 9. Phil Carrick 10. Stuart Turner 11. Craig McDermott 12. Keith Boyce 13. Fred Trueman 14. Mike Whitney 15. Vic Marks 16. Lancashire 17. Richard Ellison 18. Wasim Akram 19. Malcolm Marshall 20. Les Taylor 21. Andy Roberts 22. Jeff Thomson 23. Fred Trueman 24. Paul Jarvis 25. Sri Lanka

Singles: Abdul Qadir, Botham, Garner, Hadlee, Imran Khan, Kapil Dev and Marshall.

50. SUSSEX

1. Ian Thomson 2. Hove 3. Tony Greig 4. Geoff Greenidge 5. John Snow 6. Kepler Wessels 7. Ted Dexter 8. Ken Suttle 9. John Barclay 10. John Langridge 11. Paul Parker 12. Tony Pigott 13. Ian Greig 14. Tony Dodemaide 15. Gehan Mendis 16. Ian Gould 17. Alan Wells 18. Warwickshire 19. Ian Salisbury 20. Worcestershire 21. Garth Le Roux 22. Eastbourne 23. Neil Lenham 24. Martlets 25. Martin Speight

Singles: M Buss, Greenidge, Langridge, Parks, Tony Greig, Graves, Suttle, Griffith, A Buss, Snow and Spencer

51. ENGLAND TEST CRICKET II

1. Jack Richards 2. Australia 3. Neil Foster 4. Fred Trueman 5. Paul Allott, Jon Agnew and Ian Botham 6. John Emburey 7. Edgbaston 8. Mike Gatting 9. Jack Russell 10. India 11. Derek Pringle 12. David Steele 13. John Emburey, Mike Gatting and Paul Jarvis 14. Leslie Ames 15. Paul Terry 16. Derek Shackleton 17. John Jameson 18. Ken Barrington 19. Martyn Moxon 20. Tony Lewis 21. Peter Lever 22. Richard 23. Allan Lamb 24. Mike Hendrick 25. Norman Gifford

Singles: Amiss, Boycott, Emburey, Gooch, Hendrick, Humpage, Knott, Larkins, John Lever, Old, Sidebottom, Les Taylor, Underwood, Willey and Woolmer.

52. ENGLAND TEST CAPTAINS

1. David Gower 2. Geoff Miller 3. Tony Lewis 4. Norman Yardley 5. Sir Len Hutton 6. WG Grace 7. Peter May and Rev. David Sheppard 8. Mike Gatting 9. Bob Willis 10. Graham Gooch 11. Mike Brearley 12. Peter May 13. Dennis Lillee 14. Douglas Jardine 15. Allan Lamb 16. Raman Subba Row 17. Tony Greig 18. Christopher Cowdrey 19. Sir Jack Hobbs 20. Bob Willis 21. Johnny Douglas 22. Raymond Illingworth 23. Sir Colin Cowdrey 24. Martyn Moxon 25. Fred Titmus

Singles: Allen (Australia), Brown (Peru), Carr (Germany), Sir Colin Cowdrey (India), Dexter (Italy), Greig (South Africa), Lord Harris (Trinidad), Jardine (India), Lamb (South Africa) and Sir Pelham Warner (Trinidad).

53. GILLETTE CUP/NAT WEST TROPHY
1. Lancashire (53) **2.** Alvin Kallicharran **3.** Barry Wood **4.** Graham Gooch **5.** Middlesex **6.** Lincolnshire **7.** John Childs **8.** Warwickshire **9.** Neil Mallender **10.** Tony Greig **11.** Clive Lloyd **12.** Chris Tavare **13.** Roy and Ken Palmer and Mervyn Kitchen **14.** Yorkshire **15.** Sadiq Mohammed **16.** Curtley Ambrose **17.** Clive Lloyd, Basil D'Oliveira, Sir Colin Cowdrey, Roger Knight, Barry Wood and Tony Greig **18.** Bob Taylor **19.** Fred Trueman **20.** They beat them in a 'bowl-off' **21.** Gehan Mendis **22.** Dilip Doshi **23.** Gordon Greenidge **24.** Neal Radford **25.** Glamorgan
Singles: Leadbeater, Woodford, Close, Sharpe, Padgett, Hampshire, R Hutton, Binks, Wilson, Old and Nicholson.

54. WARWICKSHIRE
1. Lancashire **2.** Roger Twose **3.** Alan Smith **4.** Dominic Ostler, Asif Din and Andy Moles **5.** Rohan Kanhai **6.** Hong Kong **7.** MJK Smith **8.** John Whitehouse **9.** Northamptonshire **10.** Andy Lloyd **11.** South Australia **12.** Paul Smith **13.** Roger Tolchard **14.** Alan Donald **15.** David Brown **16.** Bob Willis **17.** Bombay, India **18.** David Brown **19.** Anton Ferreira **20.** Chris Old **21.** Geoff Humpage **22.** Bob Willis **23.** Leicestershire **24.** Dennis Amiss **25.** Gladstone Small
Singles: Abberley, Amiss, Brown, Gibbs, Ibadulla, Jameson, Kallicharran, Kanhai, Lewington, McVicker, Murray, Rouse, A Smith, MJK Smith, Tidy, Whitehouse and Willis.

55. CLAIM TO FAME
1. Steve O'Shaughnessy **2.** Ian Botham **3.** Old Trafford **4.** Golf **5.** Jimmy Cumbes **6.** Robin Marlar **7.** Kevin Curran **8.** Mick Malone **9.** Steve Ogrizovic **10.** Mike Gatting and Graeme Fowler **11.** David Hookes **12.** WG Grace **13.** He was the recipient of Trevor Chappell's underarm delivery that decided a one-day international **14.** Ken Barrington **15.** Lord's **16.** Mike Veletta **17.** Ted Dexter **18.** Deryck Murray **19.** Godfrey Evans **20.** Bob Willis **21.** Roger Binney **22.** Graham **23.** India **24.** Mark and Steve Waugh became the first twins to be named in the same Test match side **25.** David Boon
Singles: Allott, Botham, G Cook, Emburey, Fletcher, Gooch, Gower, Tavare, Bob Taylor, Underwood and Willis.

56. MOVING COUNTIES
1. Adam Seymour **2.** Bill Athey **3.** Surrey **4.** Steve Andrew **5.** Alan Butcher **6.** Kent and Warwickshire **7.** David Gower **8.** Phil DeFreitas **9.** Kent and Northamptonshire **10.** Derbyshire **11.** Nottinghamshire **12.** Leicestershire **13.** Simon Base **14.** Leicestershire **15.** Worcestershire **16.** Jim Love **17.** Javed Miandad **18.** Simon Hinks **19.** Trevor Jesty **20.** Bob Berry **21.** Nick Cook **22.** Stuart Fletcher **23.** Middlesex **24.** Nigel Cowley **25.** Glamorgan and Northamptonshire
Singles: Brentwood, Colchester, Ilford, Leyton, Romford and Westcliff.

ANSWERS

57. WEST INDIES

1. Roy Fredericks **2.** Andy Roberts **3.** Joel Garner **4.** Gordon Greenidge **5.** Sonny Ramadhin **6.** Clive Lloyd **7.** David Lawrence **8.** Viv Richards **9.** Colin Croft **10.** Sylvester Clarke **11.** Alvin Kallicharran **12.** Ezra Moseley **13.** David Holford **14.** Keith Arthurton **15.** Michael Holding **16.** Conrad Hunte **17.** Charlie Griffith **18.** Dennis Lillee **19.** Sir Gary Sobers **20.** Alvin Kallicharran **21.** Andy Roberts **22.** Clayton Lambert **23.** Australia **24.** Alvin Kallicharran **25.** Jeffrey Stollmeyer
Singles: Greenidge, Haynes, Richardson, Richards, Hooper, Lara, Simmons, Dujon, Logie, Marshall, Patterson, Ambrose, Allen, Williams, Walsh and Anthony.

58. WORCESTERSHIRE

1. Jimmy Cumbes **2.** Vanburn Holder **3.** Glenn Turner **4.** Phil Neale **5.** Don Kenyon **6.** Imran Khan **7.** Ted Hemsley **8.** Basil D'Oliveira **9.** Jim Standen **10.** Jack Flavell **11.** Neal Radford **12.** Dipak Patel **13.** Tim Curtis **14.** Graeme Hick **15.** Stephen Rhodes **16.** Somerset **17.** Tom Moody **18.** Stephen Rhodes **19.** Tom Moody **20.** Paul Pridgeon **21.** Norman Gifford **22.** Damian D'Oliveira **23.** Don Kenyon **24.** Gavin Haynes **25.** Hartley Alleyne
Singles: Curtis, Moody, Hick, D'Oliveira, Neale, Botham, Rhodes, Newport, Illingworth, Radford and Dilley.

59. MIXED BAG

1. Mike Denness **2.** Tony Greig **3.** Bill Frindall **4.** Fred Trueman **5.** Graham Gooch **6.** Norman Cowans **7.** There was a bomb scare **8.** Lillee was caught Willey bowled Dilley **9.** Sunil Gavaskar **10.** Mike Brearley (4310) **11.** Tom Graveney and Barry Jarman **12.** Trevor Bailey **13.** Phil Tufnell **14.** Rev. David Sheppard **15.** Pat Pocock **16.** John Crawley **17.** Bill Lawry **18.** India **19.** Sylvester Clarke **20.** Geoff Arnold **21.** Sir Len Hutton **22.** Graeme Hick **23.** Courtney Walsh **24.** Mohammed Azharuddin **25.** David Bairstow
Singles: Downton, East, French, Humpage, Parks and Richards.

60. TEST CRICKET MISCELLANY

1. Lord's **2.** Yes, they're cousins **3.** Graham Gooch **4.** John Arlott **5.** Fred Trueman and Charlie Griffith **6.** Jack Richards **7.** Zaheer Abbas **8.** New Zealand **9.** Derek Randall **10.** Robin Smith **11.** Ray Lindwall **12.** Bev Congdon **13.** Bob Holland **14.** Deryck Murray **15.** Ravi Shastri **16.** Murphy Su'a **17.** Imran Khan **18.** Rodney Marsh **19.** Mike Gatting **20.** Fred Trueman **21.** Allan Lamb **22.** Alan Oakman **23.** Dennis Amiss **24.** Dick and Peter Richardson **25.** Mudassar Nazar
Singles: Barlow, Brearley, Butcher, Daniel, Downton, Edmonds, Emburey, Gatting, Radley, Selvey and Thomson.

61. YORKSHIRE

1. David Bairstow 2. Kevin Sharp 3. Geoff Cook 4. Richard Blakey 5. Geoff Boycott 6. Don Wilson 7. Fred Trueman 8. Tony Nicholson 9. Hedley Verity 10. Phil Robinson 11. Wilfred Rhodes 12. Brian Close 13. Barrie Leadbeter 14. Geoff Cope 15. Alan Ramage 16. Graham Stevenson 17. Craig White 18. Ashley Metcalfe 19. Jimmy Binks 20. Martyn Moxon 21. Stephen Rhodes 22. Richard Blakey 23. Phil Carrick 24. Don Wilson 25. Mark Robinson
Singles: Leeds, Bradford, Sheffield, Hull, Middlesbrough, Harrogate and Scarborough.

62. TRIVIA

1. Harold Larwood 2. The players went on strike 3. CB Fry 4. Cousins 5. Hedley Verity 6. Richard Stemp 7. Robin Smith 8. To miss clashing with the eclipse of the sun 9. David Constant 10. He had ripped up Kenyan banknotes – it is an offence to deface pictures of the Kenyan President 11. It was set by twins, Mark and Steve Waugh 12. He pulled a hamstring jogging back to the hotel 13. They played Test cricket for two different countries 14. Bernard Bosanquet invented the googly, his son Reginald read the news 15. One for the choice to bat or field and one for the choice of ball (Reader or Duke) 16. They needed to catch the boat home 17. Phil DeFreitas 18. They were showing horse-racing at Ascot 19. Food poisoning 20. David Capel 21. He had been charged with manslaughter after a motoring accident 22. Ted Dexter 23. Southampton 24. Chris and Robin Smith 25. Christopher Martin-Jenkins
Singles: Buckinghamshire, Cheshire, Devon, Dorset, Hertfordshire, Ireland, Norfolk, Oxfordshire, Scotland, Shropshire, Staffordshire, Suffolk, Wales and Wiltshire.

PICTURE QUIZ ANSWERS

PICTURE QUIZ 1

1. Arundel **2.** Edgbaston **3.** Wasim Akram **4a.** Eddie Hemmings and Bruce French **4b.** Hemmings has just hit a four to give Nottinghamshire victory over Essex in the 1989 Benson & Hedges Cup final.

5. Singles: (L-R) Robinson, D Smith, L Taylor, Thomas, Edmonds, Ellison, Foster, Downton, French, Gooch, Botham, Gatting, Gower, Lamb, Willey and Emburey.

PICTURE QUIZ 2

1. Canterbury **2.** Trent Bridge **3.** Kim Barnett **4a.** Headingley **4b.** England won after following on at odds of 500/1 **4c.** Ian Botham.

5. Singles: (L-R) Base, Watkin, Capel, Alec Stewart, Stephenson, Pringle, Mickey Stewart, Lush, Roebuck, Watkinson, Hussain, Bailey, Thomas and Medlycott.

PICTURE QUIZ 3

1. Worcester **2.** Cape Town **3.** Michael Atherton **4a.** Keith Fletcher **4b.** Ravi Shastri **4c.** Fletcher, the England captain, has just shown dissent by hitting his stumps after being given out caught behind. He later apologised.

5. Singles: (L-R) B Taylor, Gatting, G Cook, J Lever, Tavare, Allott, Dilley, Emburey, Gooch, Gower, Richards, Underwood, Boycott, Fletcher, Willis, Botham.

PICTURE QUIZ 4

1. Chesterfield **2.** Old Trafford **3.** Gladstone Small **4a.** David Gower and Mike Gatting **4b.** Allan Border **4c.** Gatting thought he had caught Border but threw the ball up prematurely. The umpires decided that the fielder had not held the ball for long enough. Border went on to score 196.

5. Singles: (L-R) Jesty, Lamb, Marks, Fowler, G Cook, Pringle, Cowans, Tavare, Hemmings, Gould, Jackman, Miller, Botham, Gower, Willis, B Taylor and Randall

PICTURE QUIZ 5

1. Northampton **2.** Lord's **3.** Angus Fraser **4a.** Matthew Maynard has just been dismissed after his helmet dislodged the bails **4b.** Derbyshire and Glamorgan, Benson & Hedges semi-final 1988.

5. Two runs each: (L-R) Capel, Medlycott, Hussain, Stewart and Bailey.

HOW DID YOU SCORE?

INNINGS		
1	32	
2	33	
3	34	
4	35	
5	36	
6	37	
7	38	
8	39	
9	40	
10	41	
11	42	
12	43	
13	44	
14	45	
15	46	
16	47	
17	48	
18	49	
19	50	
20	51	
21	52	
22	53	
23	54	
24	55	
25	56	
26	57	
27	58	
28	59	
29	60	
30	61	
31	62	

PICTURE QUIZ   1
                  2
                  3
                  4
                  5

TOTAL RUN AGGREGATE _____

AVERAGE   _____

HOW DID YOU SCORE?

OVER 4000 RUNS: Marvellous. You certainly know your cricket, this is a 'Bradmanesque' performance.

3000–4000: Excellent. You have dealt with our bouncers and come out on top.

2000–3000: Good. You would hold you place in most sides.

1000–2000: Fair. We have caught you out with some tricky deliveries.

UNDER 1000: Never mind. Maybe you are better at handling out the bouncers rather than facing them.